Rick
SNA

Bruges &
Brussels

Rick Steves & Gene Openshaw

CONTENTS

INTRODUCTION

This Snapshot guide, excerpted from my guidebook *Rick Steves' Amsterdam, Bruges & Brussels,* introduces you to Belgium's top two destinations.

Bruges—once mighty, now mighty cute—comes with fancy beers in fancy glasses, lilting carillons, and lacy Gothic souvenirs of a long-gone greatness. Brussels—the capital of Europe with a Parisian ambience—has a joie de vivre, famous cuisine, a passion for comic books, and the truly grand Grand Place (Main Square), lined with cafés, chocolate shops, and Belgians living the good life. Whether you're sipping a beer or sampling a heavenly praline, rattling on your bike over the cobbles, diving into a steaming cone of Flemish (not "french") fries, gliding along a tranquil canal under fairy-tale spires, or pondering the quirky Belgian sense of humor while watching the *Manneken-Pis,* Belgium delights.

To help you have the best trip possible, I've included the following topics in this book:

• **Planning Your Time,** with advice on how to make the most of your limited time

• **Orientation,** including tourist information (abbreviated as TI), tips on public transportation, local tour options, and helpful hints

• **Sights** with ratings:

▲▲▲—Don't miss

▲▲—Try hard to see

▲—Worthwhile if you can make it

No rating—Worth knowing about

• **Self-Guided Walks** of colorful neighborhoods, and **Self-Guided Tours** of major attractions

• **Sleeping** and **Eating,** with good-value recommendations in every price range

• **Transportation Connections,** with tips on train and air travel

Practicalities, near the end of this book, has information on money, phoning, hotel reservations, transportation, and other helpful hints, plus Flemish and French survival phrases.

To travel smartly, read this little book in its entirety before you go. It's my hope that this guide will make your trip more meaningful and rewarding. Traveling like a temporary local, you'll get the absolute most out of every mile, minute, and euro.

Thanks, and have a *goede vakantie!*

Rick Steves

BELGIUM

BELGIUM

Belgium falls through the cracks. It's nestled between Germany, France, and Britain, and it's famous for waffles, sprouts, endives, and a statue of a little boy peeing—no wonder many travelers don't even consider a stop here. But many who do visit remark that Belgium is one of Europe's best-kept secrets. There are tourists—but not as many as the country's charms merit.

Belgium is split between Wallonia in the south, where they speak French, and Flanders in the north, where they speak Flemish, a dialect of Dutch. French-speakers have often dominated the government, even though about 60 percent of the population speaks Flemish. Talk to locals to learn how deep the cultural rift is. The longstanding Flemish-Dutch rivalry has become especially intense in the last couple of years. Belgium's capital, Brussels, while mostly French-speaking, is officially bilingual. The country also has a small minority of German-speaking people. Because of Brussels' international importance as the capital of the European Union, more than 25 percent of its residents are foreigners.

It's here in Belgium that Europe comes together: where Romance languages meet Germanic languages, Catholics meet Protestants, and the Benelux union was established 40 years ago, planting the seed that today is sprouting into the unification of Europe. Belgium flies the flag of Europe more vigorously than any other place on the Continent.

Bruges and Brussels are the best two first bites of Belgium. Bruges is a wonderfully preserved medieval gem that expertly nurtures its tourist industry, bringing the town a prosperity it hasn't enjoyed for 500 years, when—as one of the largest cities in the world—it helped lead northern Europe out of the Middle Ages. Brussels is simply one of Europe's great cities.

Belgians brag that they eat as much as the Germans and as

Belgium Almanac

Official Name: Royaume de Belgique/Koninkrijk België, or simply Belgique in French and België in Flemish.

Population: Of its 10.5 million people, 58 percent are Flemish, 31 percent are Walloon, and 11 percent are "mixed or other." About three-quarters are Catholic, and the rest are Protestant or other.

Latitude and Longitude: 50°N and 4°E. The latitude is similar to Alberta, Canada.

Area: With only 12,000 square miles, it's one of the smallest countries in Europe.

Geography: Belgium's flat coastal plains in the northwest and central rolling hills make it easy to invade (just ask Napoleon or Hitler). There are some rugged mountains in the southeast Ardennes Forest. The climate is temperate.

Biggest Cities: The capital city of Brussels has about 1.8 million people, followed by Antwerp's 950,000.

Economy: With few natural resources, Belgium imports most of its raw materials and exports a large volume of manufactured goods, making its economy unusually dependent on world markets. It can be a sweet business—Belgium is the world's number one exporter of chocolate. It's prosperous, with a GDP per capita of $35,350. As the "crossroads" of Europe, Brussels is the headquarters of both the EU and NATO.

Government: A parliamentary democracy, Belgium's official head of state is King Albert II. Regional tensions dominate politics: Flemish-speaking, entrepreneurial Flanders wants more autonomy, while the French-speaking "rust belt" of Wallonia is reluctant to give it. The division has made it increasingly difficult for the Belgian Parliament to form a stable coalition government. One prime minister recently said that Belgians are united only by the king, a love of beer, and the national soccer team. Voting is compulsory. More than 90 percent of registered voters participated in the last general election (compared to approximately 62 percent in the US).

Flag: Belgium's flag is composed of three vertical bands of black, yellow, and red.

The Average Belgian: The average Belgian is 42 years old—five years older than the average American—and will live to be 79. He or she is also likely to be divorced—Belgium has the highest divorce rate in Europe, with 60 for every 100 marriages. Beer is the national beverage—on average Belgians drink 26 gallons a year, just behind the Austrians and just ahead of the Brits.

BELGIUM

well as the French. They are among the world's leading beer con-
sumers and carnivores. In Belgium, never bring chrysanthemums
to a wedding—they symbolize death. And tweaking little kids on
the ear is considered rude.

Ten and a half million Belgians are packed into a country only
a little bigger than Maryland. With nearly 900 people per square
mile, it's the second most densely populated country in Europe
(after the Netherlands). This population concentration, coupled
with a dense and well-lit rail and road system, causes Belgium to
shine at night when viewed from space, a phenomenon NASA
astronauts call the "Belgian Window."

BRUGES
Brugge

ORIENTATION

With Renoir canals, pointy gilded architecture, vivid time-tunnel art, and stay-a-while cafés, Bruges is a heavyweight sightseeing destination, as well as a joy. Where else can you ride a bike along a canal, munch mussels and wash them down with the world's best beer, savor heavenly chocolate, and see Flemish Primitives and a Michelangelo, all within 300 yards of a bell tower that jingles every 15 minutes? And do it all without worrying about a language barrier?

The town is Brugge (BROO-ghah) in Flemish, and Bruges (broozh) in French and English. Its name comes from the Viking word for wharf. Right from the start, Bruges was a trading center. In the 11th century, the city grew wealthy on the cloth trade.

By the 14th century, Bruges' population was 35,000, as large as London's. As the middleman in the sea trade between northern and southern Europe, it was one of the biggest cities in the world and an economic powerhouse. In addition, Bruges had become the most important cloth market in northern Europe.

In the 15th century, while England and France were slugging it out in the Hundred Years' War, Bruges was the favored residence of the powerful Dukes of Burgundy—and at peace. Commerce and the arts boomed. The artists Jan van Eyck and Hans Memling had studios here.

But by the 16th century, the harbor had silted up and the economy had collapsed. The Burgundian court left, Belgium became a minor Habsburg possession, and Bruges' Golden Age abruptly ended. For generations, Bruges was known as a mysterious and dead city. In the 19th century, a new port, Zeebrugge, brought renewed vitality to the area. And in the 20th century, tourists discovered the town.

Today, Bruges prospers because of tourism: It's a uniquely

well-preserved Gothic city and a handy gateway to Europe. It's no secret, but even with the crowds, it's the kind of place where you don't mind being a tourist.

Bruges' ultimate sight is the town itself, and the best way to enjoy it is to get lost on the back streets, away from the lace shops and ice-cream stands.

Planning Your Time

Bruges needs at least two nights and a full, well-organized day. Even non-shoppers enjoy browsing here, and the Belgian love of life makes a hectic itinerary seem a little senseless. With one day—other than a Monday, when the three museums are closed—the speedy visitor could do the Bruges blitz described below (also included in the Bruges City Walk):

9:30 Climb the bell tower on Market Square.
10:00 Tour the sights on Burg Square.
11:30 Tour the Groeninge Museum.
13:00 Eat lunch and buy chocolates.
14:00 Take a short canal cruise.
14:30 Visit the Church of Our Lady and see Michelangelo's *Madonna and Child*.
15:00 Tour the Memling Museum.
16:00 Catch the De Halve Maan Brewery tour (note that their last tour runs at 15:00 in winter on weekdays).
17:00 Calm down in the Begijnhof courtyard.
18:00 Ride a bike around the quiet back streets of town or take a horse-and-buggy tour.
20:00 Lose the tourists and find dinner.

If this schedule seems insane, skip the bell tower and the brewery—or stay another day.

OVERVIEW

The tourist's Bruges—and you'll be sharing it—is less than one square mile, contained within a canal (the former moat). Nearly everything of interest and importance is within a convenient cobbled swath between the train station and Market Square (a 20-min walk). Many of my quiet, charming, recommended accommodations lie just beyond Market Square.

Tourist Information

The main tourist office, called **In&Uit** ("In and Out"), is in the big, red concert hall on the square called 't Zand (daily 10:00–18:00, take a number from the touch-screen machines and wait, 't Zand 34, tel. 050-448-686, www.brugge.be). The other TI is at the train

BRUGES ORIENTATION

Museum Tips

Admission prices are steep, but they include great audio-guides—so plan on spending some time and really getting into it. For information on all the museums, call 050-448-711 or visit www.brugge.be.

Combo-Tickets: The TIs and participating museums sell a museum combo-ticket (any five museums for €15, open-ended validity period). Since the Groeninge and Memling museums cost €8 each, art lovers will save money with this pass. Another combo-ticket offers any three museums and a one-day bike rental for €15 (get bike from Koffieboontje, listed under "Helpful Hints"; sold at bike shop or TI, open-ended validity period).

Blue Monday: In Bruges, nearly all museums are open Tuesday through Sunday year-round from 9:30 to 17:00 and are closed on Monday. If you're in Bruges on a Monday, the following attractions are still open: bell-tower climb on Market Square, Begijnhof, De Halve Maan Brewery Tour, Basilica of the Holy Blood, City Hall's Gothic Room, and chocolate shops and museum. You can also join a boat, bus, or walking tour, or rent a bike and pedal into the countryside.

station (Mon–Fri 10:00–17:00, Sat–Sun 10:00–14:00).

The TIs sell a great €1 *Bruges Visitors' Guide* with a map and listings of all the sights and services. You can also pick up a monthly English-language program called *events@brugge*. The TIs have information on train schedules and on the many tours available. Many hotels give out free maps with more detail than the map the TIs sell.

Arrival in Bruges

By Train: Coming in by train, you'll see the bell tower that marks the main square (Market Square, the center of town). Upon arrival, stop by the train station TI to pick up the €1 *Bruges Visitors' Guide* (with map). The station lacks ATMs, but has lockers (€3–4, daily 6:00–24:00).

The best way to get to the town center is by **bus.** Buses #1, #3, #4, #6, #11, #13, #14, and #16 (all marked *Centrum)* go directly to Market Square. Simply hop on, pay €1.60 (€1.20 if you buy in advance at train station), and in four minutes, you're there. Buses #4 and #14 continue to the northeast part of town (to the windmills and recommended accommodations on Carmersstraat). The **taxi** fare from the train station to most hotels is about €8.

It's a 20-minute **walk** from the station to the center—no fun with your luggage. If you want to walk to Market Square, cross the busy street and canal in front of the station, head up Oostmeers, and turn right on Zwidzandstraat. You can rent a **bike** at the station for the duration of your stay, but other bike rental shops are closer to the center (see "Helpful Hints," below).

By Car: Park in front of the train station in the handy two-story garage for just €2.50 for 24 hours. The parking fee includes a round-trip bus ticket into town and back for everyone in your car. There are pricier underground parking garages at the square called 't Zand and around town (€10/day, all of them well-marked). Paid parking on the street in Bruges is limited to four hours. Driving in town is very complicated because of the one-way system. The best plan for drivers: Park at the train station, visit the TI, and rent a bike or catch a bus into town.

Helpful Hints

Market Days: Bruges hosts markets on Wednesday morning (Market Square) and Saturday morning ('t Zand). On Saturday, Sunday, and public holidays, a flea market hops along Dijver in front of the Groeninge Museum. The Fish Market sells souvenirs and seafood Tuesday through Saturday mornings until 13:00.

Shopping: Shops are generally open from 10:00 to 18:00. Grocery stores are usually closed on Sunday. The main shopping street, Steenstraat, stretches from Market Square to 't Zand Square. The **Hema** department store is at Steenstraat 73 (Mon–Sat 9:00–18:00, closed Sun).

Internet Access: Punjeb Internet Shop, just a block off Market Square, is a good place to get online (€1.50/30 min, daily 10:00–22:00, 4 Philipstockstraat).

Post Office: It's on Market Square near the bell tower (Mon–Fri 9:00–18:00, Sat 9:30–12:30, closed Sun, tel. 050-331-411).

Laundry: Bruges has three self-service launderettes, each a five-minute walk from the center; ask your hotelier for the nearest one.

Bike Rental: Koffieboontje Bike Rental, just under the bell tower on Market Square, is the handiest place to rent bikes (€4/1 hr, €8/4 hrs, €12/24-hr day; special discount with this book in 2009: €8/24-hr day; free city maps and child seats, daily 9:00–22:00, Hallestraat 4, tel. 050-338-027, www.hotel -koffieboontje.be). The €15 bike-plus-any-three-museums combo-ticket works only with this outfit (and can save enough to pay for lunch).

Fietsen Popelier Bike Rental is also good (€3.50/hr, €7/4 hrs, €10/day, 24-hour day is OK if your hotel has a safe place to store bike, daily 10:00–19:00, Mariastraat 26, tel. 050-343-262). Other rental places include the less-central **De Ketting** (cheap at €5/day, daily 9:00–18:30, Gentpoortstraat 23, tel. 050-344-196, www.de ketting.be) and the **train station** (ticket window labeled *verhuring fietsen*, €9.50/day, €6.50/half-day after 14:00, €13 deposit, daily 7:00–19:30, blue lockers here for day-trippers leaving bags).

Best Town View: The bell tower overlooking Market Square rewards those who climb it with the ultimate town view.

Getting Around Bruges

Most of the city is easily walkable, but you may want to take the bus or taxi between the train station and the city center at Market Square (especially if you have heavy luggage).

By Bus: A bus ticket is good for an hour (€1.20 if you buy in advance at train station, or €1.60 on the bus). While there are various day passes, there's really no need to buy one for your visit. Nearly all city buses go directly from the train station to Market Square and fan out from there; they then return to Market Square and go back to the train station. Note that buses returning to the train station from Market Square also leave from the library bus stop, a block off the square on nearby Kuiperstraat (every 5 min). Your key: Use buses that say either *Station* or *Centrum*.

By Taxi: You'll find taxi stands at the station and on Market Square (€8/first 2 km; to get a cab in the center, call 050-334-444).

TOURS

Bruges

Bruges by Boat—The most relaxing and scenic (though not informative) way to see this city of canals is by boat, with the captain

narrating. The city carefully controls this standard tourist activity, so the many companies all offer essentially the same thing: a 30-minute route (4/hr, daily 10:00–17:00), a price of €6.50, and narration in three or four languages. Qualitative differences are because of individual guides... not companies. Always let them know you speak English to ensure you'll understand the spiel. Two companies give a €1 discount with this book: Boten Stael (just over the

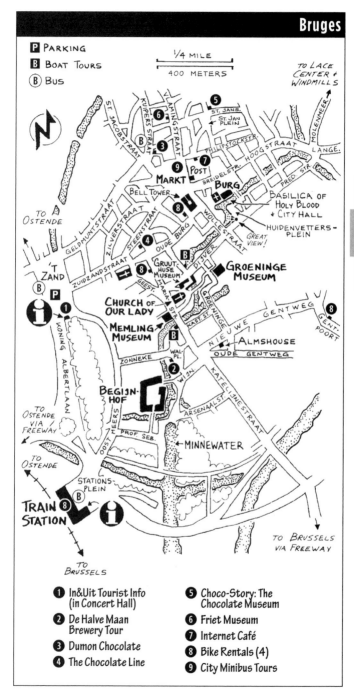

Bruges

P PARKING
B BOAT TOURS
Ⓑ BUS

¼ MILE
400 METERS

TO LACE CENTER + WINDMILLS

TO OSTENDE

'T ZAND

TO OSTENDE VIA FREEWAY

TO OSTENDE

MARKT
Bell Tower
BURG
BASILICA OF HOLY BLOOD + CITY HALL
HUIDENVETTERS-PLEIN
GREAT VIEW!

GROENINGE MUSEUM

GRUUT-HUSE MUSEUM

CHURCH OF OUR LADY

MEMLING MUSEUM

ALMSHOUSE
OUDE GENTWEG

BEGIJN-HOF

MINNEWATER

STATIONS-PLEIN

TRAIN STATION

TO BRUSSELS

TO BRUSSELS VIA FREEWAY

GENT-POORT

ST. JACOBSTRAAT
KUIPERSSTRAAT
VLAMINGSTRAAT
ST. JANS.
ST. JAN PLEIN
PHILIPSTOCKSTR.
HOOGSTRAAT
LANGE
MOLENMEER
PRED. STR.
POST
BREIDELSTR.
WOLLESTRAAT
DIJVER
GEEST
MARIA STR.
KAST. ST.
GROENINGE
NIEUWE GENTWEG
GELDMUNTSTRAAT
ZILVERSTRAAT
STEENSTRAAT
OUDE BURG
ZUIDZANDSTRAAT
ZONNEKE
WAL-PL.
WIJN.
ARSENAALST.
KATELIJNESTRAAT
OOSTMEERS
PROF. SEB.
WONING ALBERTLAAN

BRUGES ORIENTATION

❶ In&Uit Tourist Info (in Concert Hall)
❷ De Halve Maan Brewery Tour
❸ Dumon Chocolate
❹ The Chocolate Line
❺ Choco-Story: The Chocolate Museum
❻ Friet Museum
❼ Internet Café
❽ Bike Rentals (4)
❾ City Minibus Tours

canal from Memling Museum at Katelijnestraat 4, tel. 050-332-771) and Gruuthuse (Nieuwstraat 11, opposite Groeninge Museum, tel. 050-333-393).

City Minibus Tour—City Tour Bruges gives a rolling overview of the town in an 18-seat, two-skylight minibus with dial-a-language headsets and video support (€11.50, 50 min, pay driver). The tour leaves hourly from Market Square (10:00–20:00 in summer, until 18:00 in spring, until 17:00 in fall, less in winter, tel. 050-355-024, www.citytour.be). The narration, while clear, is slow-moving and a bit boring. But the tour is a lazy way to cruise past virtually every sight in Bruges.

Walking Tour—Local guides walk small groups through the core of town (€7, 2 hours, daily July–Aug, June and Sept Sat–Sun only, no tours Oct–May, depart from TI on 't Zand Square at 14:30—just drop in a few minutes early and buy tickets at the TI desk). Though earnest, the tours are heavy on history and given in two languages, so they may be less than peppy. Still, to propel you beyond the pretty gables and canal swans of Bruges, they're good medicine.

Private Guide—A private two-hour guided tour costs €60 (reserve at least one week in advance through TI, tel. 050-448-686). Or contact Christian and Danielle Scharle, who give two-hour walks for €60 and three-hour guided drives for €110 (Christian's mobile 0475-659-507, Danielle's mobile 0476-493-203, www.tourmanagementbelgium.be, tmb@skynet.be).

Horse-and-Buggy Tour—The buggies around town can take you on a clip-clop tour (€30, 35 min; price is per carriage, not per person). When divided among four or five people, this can be a good value.

Near Bruges

Quasimodo Countryside Tours—This company offers those with extra time two entertaining, all-day, English-only bus tours through the rarely visited Flemish countryside. The "Flanders Fields" tour concentrates on WWI battlefields, trenches, memorials, and poppy-splattered fields (April–Oct Tue–Sun; Nov–March Sun, Tue, and Thu only; departs at 9:15, 8 hours, visit to In Flanders Fields Museum not included). The other tour, "Triple Treat," focuses on Flanders' medieval past and rich culture, with tastes of chocolate, waffles, and beer (departs Mon, Wed, and Fri at 9:15, 8 hours). Be ready for lots of walking.

Tours cost €55, or €45 if you're under 26 (includes a picnic lunch, 9- or 30-seat bus depending on demand, non-smoking, reservations required—call tel. 050-370-470 or toll-free tel. 0800-97525, www.quasimodo.be). After making a few big-hotel pickups, the buses leave town from the Park Hotel on 't Zand Square.

Daytours—Tour guide Nathan loves leading small groups on fascinating "Flanders Fields Battlefield" day trips. This tour is like Quasimodo's (listed above), but more expensive. The differences: eight travelers on a minibus rather than a big busload; pickup from any hotel or B&B (because the small bus is allowed in the town center); restaurant lunch included rather than a picnic; and a little more serious lecturing and a stricter focus on World War I. For instance, you actually visit the In Flanders Fields Museum in Ieper—Ypres in French (€65, €3 discount when booked direct using this book, departs Tue–Sun at 9:00, 8.5 hours, call 050-346-060 or toll-free 0800-99133 to reserve, www.visitbruges.org).

Bruges by Bike—**QuasiMundo Bike Tours** leads daily five-mile bike tours around the city (English only, departs at 10:00, 2.5 hours). Their other tour, "Border by Bike," goes through the nearby countryside to Damme (March–Oct, departs at 13:00, 15 miles, 4 hours). Either tour costs €22, but you'll get €3 off with this book (tel. 050-330-775, www.quasimundo.com). Both tours include bike rental, a light raincoat (if necessary), water, and a drink in a local café. Meet on Burg Square. If

you already have a bike, you're welcome to join either tour for €14. Jos, who leads most departures, is a high-energy and entertaining guide.

Charming Mieke of **Pink Bear Bike Tours** leads small groups

on an easy and delightful 3.5-hour guided pedal along a canal to the historic town of Damme and back, finishing with a brief tour of Bruges. English tours go daily through peak season and nearly daily the rest of the year (€20, €2 discount with this book, €14 if you already have a bike, meet at 10:25 under bell tower on Market Square, tel. 050-616-686, mobile 0476-744-525, www.pinkbear.freeservers.com).

SIGHTS

These sights are listed in walking order, from Market Square, to Burg Square, to the cluster of museums around the Church of Our Lady, to the Begijnhof (10-min walk from beginning to end, without stops). For a self-guided walk and more information on each major sight, ✪ see the Bruges City Walk.

▲**Market Square (Markt)**—Ringed by a bank, the post office, lots of restaurant terraces, great old gabled buildings, and the iconic bell tower, this is the modern heart of the city (most city buses run from near here to the train station—it's a block down Kuiperstraat at the library bus stop). Under the bell tower are two great Belgian-style french-fry stands, a quadrilingual Braille description of the old town, and a metal model of the tower. In Bruges' heyday as a trading center, a canal came right up to this square. Geldmuntstraat, just off the square, is a delightful street with many fun and practical shops and eateries.

▲▲**Bell Tower (Belfort)**—Most of this bell tower has presided over Market Square since 1300, serenading passersby with carillon music. The octagonal lantern was added in 1486, making it 290 feet high—that's 366 steps. The view is worth the climb and the €5 (daily 9:30–17:00, last entry 45 min before closing, €0.40 WC in courtyard).

▲▲**Burg Square**—This opulent square is Bruges' civic center, historically the birthplace of Bruges and the site of the ninth-century castle of the first count of Flanders. Today, it's an atmospheric place to take in an outdoor concert while surrounded by six centuries of architecture.

▲**Basilica of the Holy Blood**—Originally the Chapel of Saint Basil, this church is famous for its relic of the blood of Christ, which, according to tradition, was brought to Bruges in 1150 after the Second Crusade. The lower chapel is dark and solid—a fine example of Romanesque style. The upper chapel (separate entrance, climb the stairs) is decorated Gothic. An interesting treasury museum is next to the upper chapel (treasury entry-€1.50; April–Sept Thu–Tue 9:30–12:00 & 14:00–18:00, Wed 9:30–11:45 only; Oct–March Thu–Tue 10:00–12:00 & 14:00–16:00, Wed 10:00–11:45 only; Burg Square, tel. 050-336-792, www.holyblood.com).

▲**City Hall**—This complex houses several interesting sights. Your €2.50 ticket includes an audioguide; access to a room full of old town maps and paintings; the grand, beautifully restored **Gothic Room** from 1400, starring a painted and carved wooden ceiling adorned with hanging arches (daily 9:30–17:00, Burg 12); and the less impressive **Renaissance Hall** (Brugse Vrije), basically just one ornate room with a Renaissance chimney (daily 9:30–17:00, separate entrance—in corner of square at Burg 11a).

▲▲▲**Groeninge Museum**—This museum houses a world-class collection of mostly Flemish art, from Memling to Magritte. While there's plenty of worthwhile modern art, the highlights are the vivid and pristine Flemish Primitives. ("Primitive" here means "before the Renaissance.") Flemish art is shaped by its love of detail, its merchant patrons' egos, and the power of the Church. Lose yourself in the halls of Groeninge: Gaze across 15th-century canals, into the eyes of reassuring Marys, and through town squares littered with leotards, lace, and lopped-off heads (€8, includes audioguide, Tue–Sun 9:30–17:00, closed Mon, Dijver 12, tel. 050-448-743).

○ See Groeninge Museum Tour.

Gruuthuse Museum—Once a wealthy brewer's home, this 15th-century mansion is a sprawling smattering of everything from medieval bedpans to a guillotine. A fine museum, it's now in disarray—some rooms are closed until 2011 due to an extensive reorganization and renovation (€6, includes entry to apse in Church of Our Lady, Tue–Sun 9:30–17:00, closed Mon, Dijver 17, Bruges museums tel. 050-448-711, www.brugge.be).

▲▲**Church of Our Lady**—The church stands as a memorial to the power and wealth of Bruges in its heyday. A delicate *Madonna and Child* by Michelangelo is near the apse (to the right if you're facing the altar). It's said to be the only Michelangelo statue to leave Italy in his lifetime (thanks to the wealth generated by Bruges' cloth trade). If you like tombs and church art, pay to wander through the apse (Michelangelo viewing is free, art-filled apse-€2.50, covered by €6 Gruuthuse admission or museum combo-ticket—see previous entry; church open Mon–Fri 9:30–17:00, Sat 9:30–16:45, Sun 13:30–17:00; museum and apse closed Mon; Mariastraat, www.brugge.be).

▲▲**Memling Museum/St. John's Hospital (Sint Janshospitaal)**—The former monastery/hospital complex has a fine

Bruges at a Glance

▲▲▲**Groeninge Museum** Top-notch collection of mainly Flemish art. **Hours:** Tue–Sun 9:30–17:00, closed Mon. See page 15.

▲▲**Bell Tower** Overlooking Market Square, with 366 steps to a worthwhile view and a carillon close-up. **Hours:** Daily 9:30–17:00. See page 14.

▲▲**Burg Square** Historic square with sights and impressive architecture. **Hours:** Always open. See page 14.

▲▲**Memling Museum/St. John's Hospital** Art by the greatest of the Flemish Primitives. **Hours:** Tue–Sun 9:30–17:00, closed Mon. See page 15.

▲▲**Church of Our Lady** Tombs and church art, including Michelangelo's *Madonna and Child*. **Hours:** Church open Mon–Fri 9:30–17:00, Sat 9:30–16:45, Sun 13:30–17:00 only; museum and apse closed Mon. See page 21.

▲▲**Begijnhof** Benedictine nuns' peaceful courtyard and Beguine's House museum. **Hours:** Courtyard always open, museum open daily 10:00–17:00, shorter hours off-season. See below.

▲▲**De Halve Maan Brewery Tour** Fun tour that includes beer. **Hours:** April–Oct daily on the hour 11:00–16:00, Sat until 17:00; Nov–March Mon–Fri at 11:00 and 15:00 only, Sat–Sun on the hour 11:00–16:00. See page 18.

▲▲**Biking** Exploring the countryside and pedaling to nearby Damme. **Hours:** Rental shops generally open daily 9:00–19:00. See page 20.

BRUGES SIGHTS

museum in what was once the monks' church. It contains six much-loved paintings by the greatest of the Flemish Primitives, Hans Memling. His *Mystical Wedding of St. Catherine* triptych is a highlight, as is the miniature, gilded-oak shrine to St. Ursula (€8, includes fine audioguide, Tue–Sun 9:30–17:00, closed Mon, across the street from the Church of Our Lady, Mariastraat 38, Bruges museums tel. 050-448-711, www.brugge.be).

❂ See Memling Museum Tour.

▲▲**Begijnhof**—Inhabited by Benedictine nuns, the Begijnhof courtyard (free and always open) almost makes you want to don a habit and fold your hands as you walk under its wispy trees and whisper past its frugal little homes. For a good slice of Begijnhof

▲**Market Square** Main square that is the modern heart of the city, with carillon bell tower (described on opposite page). **Hours:** Always open. See page 14.

▲**Basilica of the Holy Blood** Romanesque and Gothic church housing a relic of the blood of Christ. **Hours:** April–Sept Thu–Tue 9:30–12:00 & 14:00–18:00, Wed 9:30–11:45 only; Oct–March Thu–Tue 10:00–12:00 & 14:00–16:00, Wed 10:00–11:45 only. See page 14.

▲**City Hall** Beautifully restored Gothic Room from 1400, plus the Renaissance Hall. **Hours:** Daily 9:30–17:00. See page 15.

▲**Chocolate Shops** Bruges' specialty, sold at Dumon, The Chocolate Line, and on and on. **Hours:** Shops generally open 10:00–18:00. See page 18.

Gruuthuse Museum 15th-century mansion displaying an eclectic collection that includes furniture, tapestries, and lots more. **Hours:** Tue–Sun 9:30–17:00, closed Mon, some rooms closed until 2011. See page 15.

Choco-Story: The Chocolate Museum The whole delicious story of Belgium's favorite treat. **Hours:** Daily 10:00–17:00. See page 19.

In Flanders Fields Museum Moving WWI museum in Ypres, southwest of Bruges, easy to reach on a bus tour from Bruges. **Hours:** April–mid-Nov daily 10:00–18:00; mid-Nov–March Tue–Sun 10:00–17:00, closed Mon and for three weeks in Jan. See page 22.

BRUGES SIGHTS

life, walk through the simple museum, the Beguine's House museum (€2, daily 10:00–17:00, shorter hours off-season, English explanations, museum is left of entry gate).

Minnewater—Just south of the Begijnhof is Minnewater, an idyllic world of flower boxes, canals, and swans.

Almshouses—Walking from the Begijnhof back to the town center, you might detour along Nieuwe Gentweg to visit one of about 20 almshouses in the city. At #8, go through the door marked *Godshuis de Meulenaere 1613* into the peaceful courtyard (free). This was a medieval form of housing for the poor. The rich would pay for someone's tiny room here in return for lots of prayers.

Bruges Experiences: Beer, Chocolate, Windmills, and Biking

▲▲**De Halve Maan Brewery Tour**—Belgians are Europe's beer connoisseurs. This fun, handy tour is a great way to pay your

respects. The "Brugse Zot" is the only beer still brewed in Bruges, and the happy gang at this working-family brewery gives entertaining and informative, 45-minute tours in two languages. Avoid crowds by visiting at 11:00 or 15:00 (€5.50 includes a beer, lots of very steep steps, great rooftop panorama; tours run April–Oct daily on the hour 11:00–16:00, Sat until 17:00; Nov–March Mon–Fri 11:00 and 15:00 only, Sat–Sun on the hour 11:00–16:00; take a right down skinny Stoofstraat to #26 on Walplein, tel. 050-444-223, www .halvemaan.be).

During your tour, you'll learn that "the components of the beer are vitally necessary and contribute to a well-balanced life pattern. Nerves, muscles, visual sentience, and healthy skin are stimulated by these in a positive manner. For longevity and life-long equilibrium, drink Brugse Zot in moderation!"

Their bistro, where you'll be given your included beer, serves quick, hearty lunch plates. You can eat indoors with the smell of hops, or outdoors with the smell of hops. This is a good place to wait for your tour or to linger afterward..

▲**Chocolate Shops**—Bruggians are connoisseurs of fine chocolate. You'll be tempted by chocolate-filled display windows all over town. While Godiva is the best big-factory/high-price/high-quality brand, there are plenty of smaller, family-run places in Bruges that offer exquisite handmade chocolates. Both of the following chocolatiers are proud of their creative varieties, generous with their samples, and welcome you to assemble a 100-gram assortment of five or six chocolates.

Dumon: Perhaps Bruges' smoothest and creamiest chocolates are at Dumon (€2.10/100 grams). Madame Dumon and her children (Stefaan, Natale, and Christophe) make their top-notch chocolate daily and sell it fresh just off Market Square (Thu–Tue 10:00–18:00, closed Wed, old chocolate molds on display in

basement, Eiermarkt 6, tel. 050-346-282). The Dumons don't provide English labels because they believe it's best to describe their chocolates in person—and they do it with an evangelical fervor. Try a small mix-and-match box to sample a few out-of-this-world flavors, and come back for more of your favorites.

The Chocolate Line: Locals and tourists alike flock to The Chocolate Line (pricey at €4.40/100 grams) to taste the *gastronomique* varieties concocted by Dominique Person—the mad scientist of chocolate. His unique creations include Havana cigar (marinated in rum, cognac, and Cuban tobacco leaves—so therefore technically illegal in the US), lemongrass, lavender, ginger (shaped like a Buddha), saffron curry, spicy chili, and Moroccan mint. New combinations from Dominique's imagination are a Pop Rocks/cola chocolate, as well as "wine vinegar" chocolate (surprisingly good). The kitchen—busy whipping up 80 varieties—is on display in the back. Enjoy the window display, renewed monthly (daily 9:30–18:00, between Church of Our Lady and Market Square at Simon Stevinplein 19, tel. 050-341-090).

Choco-Story: The Chocolate Museum—This museum is rated ▲ for chocoholics. The Chocolate Fairy leads you through 2,600 years of chocolate history—explaining why, in the ancient

Mexican world of the Mayas and the Aztecs, chocolate was considered the drink of the gods, and cocoa beans were used as a means of payment. With lots of artifacts well-described in English, the museum fills you in on the production of truffles, bonbons, hollow figures, and solid bars of chocolate. Then you'll view a delicious little video (8 min long, repeating continuously, alternating Flemish, French, and then English; peek into the theater to check the schedule. If you have time before the next English showing, visit the exhibits in the top room). Your finale is in the "demonstration room," where—after a 10-minute cooking demo—you get a taste (€6, €10 combo-ticket includes nearby Friet Museum, daily 10:00–17:00; where Wijnzakstraat meets Sint Jansstraat at Sint Jansplein, 3-min walk from Market Square; tel. 050-612-237, www.choco-story.be).

Friet Museum—It's the only place in the world that enthusiastically tells the story of french fries, which, of course, aren't even French—they're Belgian. As there are no real artifacts, you could just Google it and save the €6 entry fee (€10 combo-ticket includes Chocolate Museum, daily 10:00–17:00, Vlamingstraat 33, tel. 050-340-150, www.frietmuseum.be).

Windmills and Lace by the Moat—A 15-minute walk from the center to the northeast end of town brings you to four windmills strung along a pleasant grassy setting on the "big moat" canal. The St. Janshuysmolen **windmill** is open to visitors (€2, May–Aug daily 9:30–12:30 & 13:30–17:00, closed Sept–April, at the end of Carmersstraat, between Kruispoort and Dampoort, on Bruges side of the moat).

The **Folklore Museum,** in the same neighborhood, is cute but forgettable (€2, Tue–Sun 9:30–12:30 & 13:30–17:00, closed Mon, Balstraat 43, tel. 050-448-764). To find it, ask for the Jerusalem Church. On the same street is a lace shop with a good reputation—'t **Apostelientje** (Mon–Fri 9:30–18:00, Sat 10:00–17:00, Sun 10:00–13:00, Balstraat 11, tel. 050-337-860).

▲▲**Biking**—The Flemish word for bike is *fiets* (pronounced "feets"). While Bruges' sights are close enough for easy walking, the town is a treat for bikers, and a bike quickly gets you into dreamy back lanes without a hint of tourism. Take a peaceful evening ride through the town's nooks and crannies and around the outer canal. Consider keeping a bike for the duration of your stay—it's the way the locals get around in Bruges. Along the canal that circles the town, there is now a park with a delightful bike lane. Rental shops have maps and ideas.

⊙ **Self-Guided Bike Ride to Damme:** For the best short bike trip out of Bruges, rent a bike and pedal four miles to the nearby town of Damme. You'll enjoy a whiff of the countryside and see a working windmill while riding along a canal to this interesting city. Allow about two hours for the leisurely round-trip bike ride and a brief stop in Damme. The Belgium/Netherlands border is a 40-minute pedal (along the same canal) beyond Damme.

• *Head east from Bruges' Market Square through Burg Square and out to the canal. (You could stop to see the Jerusalem Church and a lace shop on the way—described above.) At the canal, circle to the left, passing several windmills (one is open for viewing, described above). At the last windmill, named Dampoort, head away from Bruges on the left (north) side of the Damme Canal, via Noorweegse Kaai/ Damse Vaart-West.*

The Damme Canal: From Dampoort, you'll pedal straight and level along the canal directly to Damme. There's no opportunity to cross the canal until you reach the town. The farmland to your left is a *polder*—a salt marsh that flooded each spring, until it was reclaimed by industrious local farmers. The Damme Canal, also called the Napoleon Canal, was built in 1811 by Napoleon (actually by his Spanish prisoners) in a failed attempt to reinvigorate the city as a port. Today locals fish this canal for eels and wait for the next winter freeze. Old-timers have fond memories of skating to Holland on this canal—but it hasn't had a hard freeze for over a decade.

Windmill: Just before arriving in Damme, you'll come upon a working windmill that dates from 1867. More clever than the windmills in Bruges, this one is designed so just the wood cap turns to face the wind—rather than the entire building. If it's open, climb up through the creaking, spinning, wind-powered gears to the top floor (free, Sat–Sun 9:30–18:00).

In its day (13th–15th centuries), Bruges was one of the top five European ports and little Damme was important as well. Today all you see is land—the once-bustling former harbors silted up, causing the sea to retreat. Pause atop the bridge just beyond the windmill. From here you can see how, at Napoleon's instructions, the canal was designed to mimic a grand Parisian boulevard, leading to the towering Church of Our Lady back in Bruges.

• *From here the canal continues straight to Holland. (If tempted...you're a third of the way to the border.) Cross the bridge and follow Kerkstraat, which cuts through the center of town, to Damme's main square and City Hall.*

Damme: Once a thriving medieval port, and then a moated garrison town, today Damme is a tourist center—a tiny version of Bruges. It has a smaller-but-similar City Hall, a St. John's Hospital, and a big brick Church of Our Lady. You can tell by its 15th-century City Hall that, 500 years ago, Damme was rolling in herring money. Rather than being built with Belgian bricks (like other buildings around here), the City Hall was made of French limestone. Originally the ground floor was a market and fish warehouse, with government offices upstairs.

• *Continue on Kerkstraat as it leads two blocks farther to the Church of Our Lady. Along the way, you could side-trip to the left, down Pottenbakkersstraat, which takes you to a quaint little square called Haringmarkt (named for the Herring Market that made Damme rich in the 15th century). The trees you see from here mark the lines of the town's long-gone, 17th-century ramparts. Returning to Kerkstraat, continue on to the big church.*

The Church of Our Lady: This church, which rose and fell with the fortunes of Damme, dates from the 13th century. Inside are two Virgin Marys: To the right of the altar, a 1630 wooden statue of Mary, and to the left, Our Lady of the Fishermen (c. 1650, in a glass case). Over the nave stands Belgium's oldest wooden statue, St. Andrew, with his X-shaped cross.

Outside, under the 13th-century church tower, is a three-faced, modern fiberglass sculpture by the Belgian artist Charles Delporte. Called *View of Light,* it evokes three lights: morning (grace), mid-day (kindness), and evening (gentleness). If you like his work, there's more at his nearby gallery.

• *To return to Bruges, continue past the church on Kerkstraat. Just before crossing the next bridge, follow a dirt lane to the right that leads scenically back to the Damme Canal (and Damse Vaart-Zuid). Take this road back to Bruges.*

Near Bruges

In Flanders Fields Museum—This World War I museum, about 40 miles southwest of Bruges, provides a moving look at the battles fought near Ieper (Ypres in French), where British losses totaled 60,000 dead and wounded in five weeks. Use its interactive computer displays to trace the wartime lives of individual soldiers and citizens. Powerful videos and ear-shattering audio complete the story (€8; April–mid-Nov daily 10:00–18:00; mid-Nov–March Tue–Sun 10:00–17:00, closed Mon and for three weeks in Jan; last entry one hour before closing, Grote Markt 34, Ieper, tel. 057-239-220, www.inflandersfields.be). From Bruges, catch a train to Ieper via Kortrijk (2 hrs), or take a tour. Drivers take E-403 to Kortrijk, then A-19 to Ieper, following signs to *Bellewaerde.*

BRUGES CITY WALK

This walk, which takes you from Market Square to the Burg to the cluster of museums around the Church of Our Lady (the Groeninge, Gruuthuse, and Memling), shows you the best of Bruges in a day.

ORIENTATION

Length of This Walk: Allow two hours for the walk, plus time for Bruges' two big museums (Groeninge and Memling).

Bell Tower (Belfort): €5, daily 9:30–17:00, last entry 45 min before closing, on Market Square.

Basilica of the Holy Blood: Treasury entry-€1.50; April–Sept Thu–Tue 9:30–12:00 & 14:00–18:00, Wed 9:30–11:45 only; Oct–March Thu–Tue 10:00–12:00 & 14:00–16:00, Wed 10:00–11:45 only; Burg Square, tel. 050-336-792, www.holy blood.com.

City Hall's Gothic Room: €2.50, includes audioguide and entry to Renaissance Hall, daily 9:30–17:00, Burg 12.

Renaissance Hall (Brugse Vrije): €2.50, includes audioguide and admission to City Hall's Gothic Room, daily 9:30–17:00, entrance in corner of square at Burg 11a.

Groeninge Museum: €8, includes audioguide, Tue–Sun 9:30–17:00, closed Mon, Dijver 12, tel. 050-448-743.

Gruuthuse Museum: €6, includes entry to apse of Church of Our Lady, Tue–Sun 9:30–17:00, closed Mon, some rooms closed until 2011, Dijver 17, Bruges museums tel. 050-448-711.

Church of Our Lady: Free peek at Michelangelo sculpture, €2.50 for art-filled apse, covered by €6 Gruuthuse admission or museum combo-ticket; church open Mon–Fri 9:30–17:00, Sat 9:30–16:45, Sun 13:30–17:00 only; museum and apse closed

Mon, Mariastraat.

Memling Museum: €8, includes fine audioguide, Tue–Sun 9:30–17:00, closed Mon, Mariastraat 38.

De Halve Maan Brewery Tour: €5 tour includes a beer; April–Oct daily on the hour 11:00–16:00, Sat until 17:00; 11:00 and 15:00 are best to avoid groups; Nov–March Mon–Fri at 11:00 and 15:00 only, Sat–Sun on the hour 11:00–16:00; take a right down narrow Stoofstraat to #26 on Walplein, tel. 050-444-223, www.halvemaan.be.

Begijnhof: Courtyard free and always open; Beguine's House museum costs €2, open daily 10:00–17:00, shorter hours off-season.

THE WALK BEGINS

Market Square (Markt)

Ringed by the post office, lots of restaurant terraces, great old gabled buildings, and the bell tower, this is the modern heart of the city. And, in Bruges' heyday as a trading city, this was also the center. The "typical" old buildings here were rebuilt in the 19th century in an exaggerated Neo-Gothic style (Bruges is often called "more Gothic than Gothic"). This pre–Martin Luther style was a political statement for this Catholic town.

Formerly, a canal came right up to this square. Imagine boats moored where the post office stands today. In the 1300s, farm-

ers shipped their cotton, wool, flax, and hemp to the port at Bruges. Before loading it onto outgoing boats, the industrious locals would spin, weave, and dye it into a finished product.

By 1400, the economy was shifting away from textiles and toward more refined goods, such as high-fashion items, tapestry, chairs, jewelry, and paper—a new invention (replacing parchment) that was made in Flanders with cotton that was shredded, soaked, and pressed.

The square is adorned with **flags,** including the red-white-and-blue lion flag of Bruges, the black-yellow-and-red flag of Belgium, and the blue-with-circle-of-yellow-stars flag of the European Union.

The **statue** depicts two friends, Jan Breidel and Pieter de Coninc, clutching sword and shield and looking towards France as they led a popular uprising against the French king in 1302. The rebels identified potential French spies by demanding they

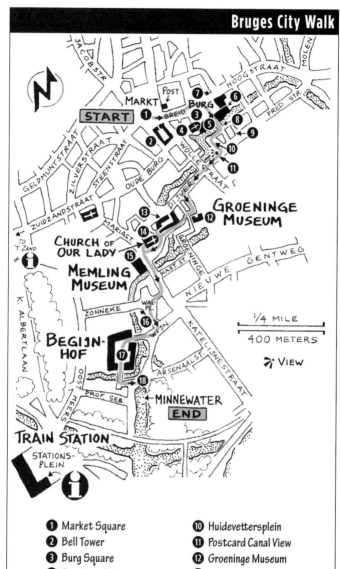

Bruges City Walk

1 Market Square
2 Bell Tower
3 Burg Square
4 Basilica of the Holy Blood
5 City Hall
6 Renaissance Hall
7 Crowne Plaza Hotel
8 Blinde Ezelstraat
9 Fish Market
10 Huidevettersplein
11 Postcard Canal View
12 Groeninge Museum
13 Gruuthuse Museum
14 Church of Our Lady
15 Memling Museum
16 De Halve Maan Brewery
17 Begijnhof
18 Minnewater

repeat two words—*schild en vriend* (shield and friend)—that only Flemish locals (or foreigners with phlegm) could pronounce. They won Flanders its freedom. Cleverly using hooks to pull knights from their horses, they scored the medieval world's first victory of foot soldiers over cavalry, and of common people over nobility. The French knights, thinking that fighting these Flemish peasants would be a cakewalk, had worn their dress uniforms. The peasants had a field day afterward scavenging all the golden spurs from the fallen soldiers after the Battle of the Golden Spurs (1302).

Geldmuntstraat, a block west of the square, has fun shops and eateries. Steenstraat is the main shopping street and is packed with people. Want a coffee? Stop by the Café-Brasserie Craenenburg on Market Square. Originally the house where Maximilian of Austria was imprisoned in 1488, it's been a café since 1905 (daily 7:30–24:00, Markt 16).

Bell Tower (Belfort)

Most of this bell tower has stood over Market Square since 1300. The octagonal lantern was added in 1486, making it 290 feet high. The tower combines medieval crenellations, pointed Gothic arches,

round Roman arches, flamboyant spires, and even a few small flying buttresses (two-thirds of the way up).

Try some Belgian-style fries from either stand at the bottom of the tower. Look for the small metal model of the tower and the Braille description of the old town. Enter the courtyard. At the base of the bell tower, find the posted schedule of free carillon concerts (normally June–Sept Mon, Wed, and Sat at 21:00; Oct–May Wed and Sun at 14:15, sit on benches in courtyard—a great experience). There's also a WC in the courtyard (€0.40).

Climb the tower (€5, 366 steps). Just before you reach the top, peek into the carillon room. The 47 bells can be played mechanically with the giant barrel and movable tabs (as they are on each quarter hour), or with a manual keyboard (as they are during concerts). The carillonneur uses his fists and feet, rather than fingers. Be there on the

quarter hour, when things ring. It's *bellissimo* at the top of the hour.

Atop the tower, survey Bruges. On the horizon, you can see the towns along the North Sea coast.

• *Leaving the bell tower, turn right (east) onto Breidelstraat, and thread yourself through the lace and waffles to Burg Square.*

Burg Square

This opulent square is Bruges' historical birthplace, political center, and religious heart. Today it's the scene of outdoor concerts and local festivals.

Pan the square to see six centuries of architecture. Starting with the view of the bell tower above the gables, sweep counterclockwise 360 degrees. You'll go from Romanesque (the interior of the fancy, gray-brick **Basilica of the Holy Blood** in the corner), to the pointed Gothic arches and prickly steeples of the white sandstone **City Hall,** to the well-proportioned Renaissance windows of the **Old Recorder's House** (next door, under the gilded statues), to the elaborate 17th-century Baroque of the **Provost's House** (past the park behind you). The **park** at the back of the square is the site of a cathedral that was demolished during the French Revolutionary period. Today, the foundation is open to the public in the **Crowne Plaza Hotel** basement. The modern, Japanese-designed **fountain** plays with motifs of lace and water, but locals simply call it "the car wash."

• *Complete your spin and walk to the small, fancy, gray-and-gold building in the corner of Burg Square.*

Basilica of the Holy Blood

The gleaming gold knights and ladies on the church's gray facade remind us that this double-decker church was built (c. 1150) by a brave Crusader to house the drops of Christ's blood he'd brought back from Jerusalem.

Lower Chapel: Enter the lower chapel through the door labeled *Basiliek.* Inside, the stark and dim decor reeks of the medieval piety that drove crusading Christian Europeans to persecute Muslims. With heavy columns and round arches, the style is pure Romanesque. The annex along

The Legend of the Holy Blood

Several drops of Christ's blood, washed from his lifeless body by Joseph of Arimathea, were preserved in a rock-crystal vial in Jerusalem. In 1150, the patriarch of Jerusalem gave the blood to a Flemish soldier, Derrick of Alsace, as thanks for rescuing his city from the Muslims during the Second Crusade. Derrick (also called Dedric or Thierry) returned home and donated it to the city. The old, dried blood suddenly turned to liquid, a miracle repeated every Friday for the next two centuries, and verified by thousands of pilgrims from around Europe who flocked here to adore it. The blood dried up for good in 1325.

Every year on Ascension Day (May 21 in 2009, May 13 in 2010), Bruges' bankers, housewives, and waffle vendors put on old-time costumes for the parading of the vial through the city. Crusader knights re-enact the bringing of the relic, Joseph of Arimathea washes Christ's body, and ladies in medieval costume with hair tied up in horn-like hairnets come out to wave flags, while many Bruges citizens just take the day off.

the right aisle displays somber statues of Christ being tortured and entombed, plus a 12th-century relief panel over a doorway showing St. Basil (a fourth-century scholarly monk) being baptized by a double-jointed priest, and a man-size dove of the Holy Spirit.

• *Go back outside and up the staircase to reach the...*

Upper Chapel: After being gutted by Napoleon's secular-humanist crusaders in 1797, the upper chapel's original Romanesque

decor was redone in a Neo-Gothic style. The nave is colorful, with a curved wooden ceiling, painted walls, and stained-glass windows of the dukes who ruled Flanders, along with their duchesses.

The painting at the main altar tells how the Holy Blood got here. Derrick of Alsace, having helped defend Jerusalem *(Hierosolyma)* and Bethlehem *(Bethlema)* from Muslim incursions in the Second Crusade, kneels (left) before the grateful Christian patriarch of Jerusalem, who rewards him with the relic. Derrick returns home (right) and kneels before Bruges' bishop to give him the vial of blood.

The relic itself—some red stuff preserved inside a clear, six-inch tube of rock crystal—is kept in the adjoining room (through the three arches). It's in the tall, silver tabernacle on the altar. (Each

Friday—and increasingly on other days, too—the tabernacle's doors will be open, so you can actually see the vial of blood.) On holy days, the relic is shifted across the room and displayed on the throne under the canopy.

Treasury (next to Upper Chapel): For €1.50, you can see the impressive gold-and-silver, gem-studded, hexagonal reliquary (c. 1600, left wall) that the vial of blood is  paraded around in on feast days. The vial is placed in the "casket" at the bottom of the four-foot-tall structure. On the wall, flanking the shrine, are paintings of kneeling residents who, for centuries, have tended the shrine and organized the pageantry as part of the 31-member Brotherhood of the Holy Blood. Elsewhere in the room are the Brothers' ceremonial necklaces, clothes, chalices, and so on.

In the display case by the entrance, find the lead box that protected the vial of blood from Protestant extremists (1578) and French Revolutionaries (1797) bent on destroying what, to them, was a glaring symbol of Catholic mumbo-jumbo. The broken rock-crystal tube with gold caps on either end is a replica of the vial, giving an idea of what the actual relic looks like. Opposite the reliquary are the original cartoons (from 1541) that provided the designs for the basilica's stained glass.

City Hall (Stadhuis)

Built in about 1400, when Bruges was a thriving bastion of capitalism with a population of 35,000, this building served as a model for town halls elsewhere, including Brussels. The white sand-

stone facade is studded with statues of knights, nobles, and saints with prickly Gothic steeples over their heads. A colorful double band of cities' coats of arms includes those of Bruges (Brugghe) and Dunkirk (Dunquerke). Back then, Bruges' jurisdiction included many towns in present-day France. The building is still the City Hall, and it's not unusual to see couples arriving here to get married.

Entrance Hall: The ground-level lobby (free, closed Mon) leads to a picture gallery with scenes from Belgium's history, from the Spanish king to the arrival of Napoleon, shown meeting the mayor here at the City Hall in 1803.

• *You can pay to climb the stairs for a look at the...*

Gothic Room: Some of modern democracy's roots lie in this ornate room, where, for centuries, the city council met to discuss the town's affairs (€2.50 entry includes audioguide—which explains both the upstairs and the ground floor—and entrance to the adjacent Renaissance Hall). In 1464, one of Europe's first parliaments, the Estates General of the Low Countries, convened here. The fireplace at the far end bears a proclamation from 1305, which says, "All the artisans, laborers...and citizens of Bruges are free—all of them" (provided they pay their taxes).

The elaborately carved and painted wooden ceiling (a Neo-Gothic reconstruction from the 19th century) features tracery in gold, red, and black. Five dangling arches ("pendentives") hang down the center, now adorned with modern floodlights. Notice the New Testament themes carved into the circular medallions that decorate the points where the arches meet.

The **wall murals** are late-19th-century Romantic paintings depicting episodes in the city's history. Start with the biggest painting along the left wall, and work clockwise, following the numbers found on the walls:

1. Hip, hip, hooray! Everyone cheers, flags wave, trumpets blare, and dogs bark, as Bruges' knights, dressed in gold with black Flemish lions, return triumphant after driving out French oppressors and winning Flanders' independence. The Battle of the Golden Spurs (1302) is remembered every July 11.

2. Bruges' high-water mark came perhaps at this elaborate ceremony, when Philip the Good of Burgundy (seated, in black) assembled his court here in Bruges and solemnly founded the knightly Order of the Golden Fleece (1429).

3. The Crusader knight, Derrick of Alsace, returns from the Holy Land and kneels at the entrance of St. Basil's Chapel to present the relic of Christ's Holy Blood (c. 1150).

4. A nun carries a basket of bread in this scene from St. John's Hospital.

5. A town leader stands at the podium and hands a sealed document to a German businessman, renewing the Hanseatic League's business license. Membership in this club of trading cities was a key to Bruges' prosperity.

6. As peasants cheer, a messenger of the local duke proclaims the town's right to self-government (1190).

7. The mayor visits a Bruges painting studio to shake the

hand of Jan van Eyck, the great Flemish Primitive painter (1433). Jan's wife, Margareta, is there, too. In the 1400s, Bruges rivaled Florence and Venice as Europe's cultural capital. See the town in the distance, out Van Eyck's window.

8. Skip it.

9. City fathers grab a ceremonial trowel from a pillow to lay the fancy cornerstone of the City Hall (1376). Bruges' familiar towers stand in the background.

10. Skip it.

11. It's a typical market day at the Halls (the courtyard behind the bell tower). Arabs mingle with Germans in fur-lined coats and beards in a market where they sell everything from armor to lemons.

12. A bishop blesses a new canal (1404) as ships sail right by the city. This was Bruges in its heyday, before the silting of the harbor. At the far right, the two bearded men with moustaches are the brothers who painted these murals.

In the adjoining room, old paintings and maps show how little the city has changed through the centuries. A map (on the right

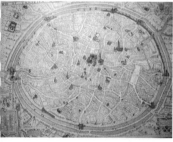

wall) shows in exquisite detail the city as it looked in 1562. (The map is oriented with south on top.) Find the bell tower, the Church of Our Lady, and Burg Square, which back then was bounded on the north by a cathedral. Notice the canal (on the west) leading from the North Sea right to Market Square. A moat encircled the city with its gates, unfinished wall, and 28 windmills (four of which survive today). The mills pumped water to the town's fountains, made paper, ground grain, and functioned as the motor of the Middle Ages. Most locals own a copy of this map that shows how their neighborhood looked 400 years ago.

• *Back on the square, leaving the City Hall, turn right and go to the corner.*

Renaissance Hall (Brugse Vrije)

This elaborately decorated room has a grand Renaissance chimney carved from oak by Bruges' Renaissance man, Lancelot Blondeel, in 1531. If you're into heraldry, the symbolism makes this room worth a five-minute stop. If you're not, you'll wonder

BRUGES CITY WALK

where the rest of the museum is.

The centerpiece of the incredible carving is the Holy Roman Emperor Charles V. The hometown duke, on the far left, is related to Charles V. By making the connection to the Holy Roman Emperor clear, this carved family tree of Bruges' nobility helped substantiate their power. Notice the closely guarded family jewels. And check out the expressive little cherubs.

Crowne Plaza Hotel

One of the city's newest buildings (1992) sits atop the ruins of the town's oldest structures. In about A.D. 900, when Viking ships regularly docked here to rape and pillage, Baldwin Iron Arm built a fort *(castrum)* to protect his Flemish people. In 950, the fort was converted into St. Donatian's Church, which became one of the city's largest.

Ask politely at the hotel's reception desk to see the archaeological site—ruins of the fort and the church—in the basement. If there's no conference in progress, they'll let you walk down the stairs and have a peek.

In the basement of the modern hotel are conference rooms lined with old stone walls and display cases of objects found in the ruins of earlier structures. On the immediate left hangs a photo of a document announcing the *Vente de Materiaux* (sale of material). When Napoleon destroyed the church in the early 1800s, its bricks were auctioned off. A local builder bought them at auction, and now the pieces of the old cathedral are embedded in other buildings throughout Bruges.

See oak pilings, carved to a point, once driven into this former peat bog to support the fort and shore up its moat. Paintings show the immensity of the church that replaced it. The curved stone walls you walk among are from the foundations of the ambulatory around the church altar.

Excavators found a town water hole—a bonanza for archaeologists—turning up the refuse of a thousand years of habitation: pottery, animal skulls, rosary beads, dice, coins, keys, thimbles, pipes, spoons, and Delftware.

Don't miss the 14th-century painted sarcophagi—painted quickly for burial, with the crucifixion on the west end and the Virgin and Child on the east.

• Back on Burg Square, walk south under the Goldfinger family (through the small archway) down the alleyway called...

Blinde Ezelstraat

Midway down on the left side (knee level), see an original iron hinge from the city's south gate, back when the city was ringed by a moat and closed nightly at 22:00. On the right wall, at eye level, a black patch shows just how grimy the city had become before a 1960s cleaning. Despite the cleaning and a few fanciful reconstructions, the city looks today much as it did in centuries past.

The name "Blinde Ezelstraat" means "Blind Donkey Street." In medieval times, the donkeys, carrying fish from the North Sea on their backs, were stopped here so that their owners could put blinders on them. Otherwise, the donkeys wouldn't cross the water between the old city and the fish market.

• *Cross the bridge over what was the 13th-century city moat. On your left are the arcades of the...*

Fish Market (Vismarkt)

The North Sea is just 12 miles away, and the fresh catch is sold here (Tue–Sat 6:00–13:00). Once a thriving market, today it's mostly souvenirs...and the big catch is the tourists.

• *Take an immediate right (west), entering a courtyard called...*

Huidevettersplein

This tiny, picturesque, restaurant-filled square was originally the headquarters of the town's skinners and tanners. On the facade of the Hotel Duc de Bourgogne, four old relief panels show scenes from the leather trade—once a leading Bruges industry. First, they tan the hide in a bath of acid; then, with tongs, they pull it out to dry; then they beat it to make it soft; and finally, they scrape and clean it to make it ready for sale.

• *Continue a few steps to Rozenhoedkaai street, where you can look back to your right and get a great...*

Postcard Canal View

The bell tower reflected in a quiet canal lined with old houses—this view is the essence of Bruges. Seeing buildings rising straight

from the water makes you understand why this was the Venice of the North. Can you see the bell tower's tilt? It leans about four feet. The tilt has been carefully monitored since 1740, but no change has been detected.

To your left (west) down the Dijver canal (past a flea market on weekends) looms the huge spire of the Church of Our Lady, the tallest brick spire in the Low Countries. Between you and the church are the Europa College (a postgraduate institution for training future "Eurocrats" about the laws, economics, and politics of the European Union) and two fine museums.

BRUGES CITY WALK

• *Continue walking with the canal and bell tower on your right. About 100 yards ahead, on the left, is the copper-colored sign that points the way to the...*

Groeninge Museum

This sumptuous collection of paintings takes you from 1400 to 1945. The highlights are its Flemish Primitives, with all their glorious detail.

○ See Groeninge Museum Tour.

• *Leaving the Groeninge, take your first left, into a courtyard. You'll see the prickly church steeple ahead. Head up and over the picture-perfect 19th-century pedestrian bridge.*

From the bridge, look up at the corner of the Gruuthuse mansion, where there's a teeny-tiny window, a toll-keeper's lookout. The bridge gives you a close-up look at Our Lady's big buttresses and round apse. Go slightly right, between the two huge buildings. On the right is a large stone courtyard, where you'll find the entrance to the...

Gruuthuse Museum

This 15th-century mansion of a wealthy Bruges merchant displays period furniture, tapestries, coins, and musical instruments. Extensive renovation will have this museum in a disappointing state of disarray until 2011. Use the leaflets in each room to browse through a collection of secular objects that are both functional and beautiful. Here are some highlights:

On the left, in the first room (or **Great Hall**), the big fireplace, oak table, and tapestries attest to the wealth of Louis Gruuthuse, who got rich providing a special herb used to spice up beer.

Tapestries like the ones you see here were a famous Flemish export product, made in local factories out of raw wool imported from England and silk brought from the Orient (via Italy). Both beautiful and useful (as insulation), they adorned many homes and palaces throughout Europe.

The Gruuthuse mansion abuts the Church of Our Lady and has a convenient little **chapel** (upstairs via the far corner of Room 16) with a window overlooking the interior of the huge church. In their private box seats above the choir, the family could attend services without leaving home. From the balcony, you can look down on two reclining gold statues in the church, marking the tombs of Charles the Bold and his daughter, Mary of Burgundy (the grandmother of powerful Charles V).

Leaving the museum, contemplate the mountain of bricks

that towers 400 feet above, as it has for 600 years. You're heading for that church.

• *Walk left out of the courtyard, doubling back the way you came, toward the pedestrian bridge. But this time, go right after the archway, circling clockwise around the outside of the church. Ahead on the right is the entrance to the...*

Church of Our Lady

This church stands as a memorial to the power and wealth of Bruges in its heyday.

A delicate ***Madonna and Child by Michelangelo*** (1504) is near the apse (to the right as you enter), somewhat overwhelmed by the ornate Baroque niche it sits in. It's said to be the only Michelangelo statue to leave Italy in his lifetime, bought in Tuscany by a wealthy Bruges businessman, who's buried beneath it.

As Michelangelo chipped away at the masterpiece of his youth, *David,* he took breaks by carving this one in 1504. Mary,

slightly smaller than life-size, sits, while young Jesus stands in front of her. Their expressions are mirror images—serene, but a bit melancholy, with downcast eyes, as though pondering the young child's dangerous future. Though they're lost in thought, their hands instinctively link, tenderly. The white Carrara marble is highly polished, something Michelangelo only did when he was certain he'd gotten it right.

If you like tombs and church art, pay €2.50 to wander through the apse (also covered by €6 Gruuthuse admission and museum combo-ticket). The highlight is the reclining statues marking the tombs of the last local rulers of Bruges, Mary of Burgundy, and her father, Charles the Bold. The dog and lion at their feet are symbols of fidelity and courage.

In 1482, when 25-year-old Mary of Burgundy tumbled from a horse and died, she left behind a toddler son and a husband who was heir to the Holy Roman Empire. Beside her lies her father, Charles the Bold, who also died prematurely, in war. Their twin deaths meant Bruges belonged to Austria, and would soon be swallowed up by the empire and ruled from afar by Habsburgs—who didn't understand or care about its problems. Trade routes shifted, and goods soon flowed through Antwerp, then Amsterdam, as Bruges' North Sea port silted up. After these developments, Bruges began four centuries of economic decline. The city was eventually mothballed. It was later discovered by modern-day tourists to be remarkably well-pickled—which explains its current affluence.

The balcony to the left of the main altar is part of the Gruuthuse mansion next door, providing the noble family with prime seats for Mass.

Excavations in 1979 turned up fascinating grave paintings on the tombs below and near the altar. Dating from the 13th century, these show Mary represented as Queen of Heaven (on a throne, carrying a crown and scepter) and Mother of God (with the baby Jesus on her lap). Since Mary is in charge of advocating with Jesus for your salvation, she's a good person to have painted on the wall of your tomb. Tombs also show lots of angels—generally patron saints of the dead person—swinging thuribles (incense burners).

• *Just across Mariastraat from the church entrance is the entry to the St. John's Hospital's Visitors Center (with a good Internet café and a €0.30 public WC). The entrance to the Memling Museum, which fills that hospital's church, is 20 yards south (to the left) on Mariastraat.*

Memling Museum

This medieval hospital contains some much-loved paintings by the greatest of the Flemish Primitives, Hans Memling. His *Mystical Wedding of St. Catherine* triptych deserves a close look. Catherine and her "mystical groom," the baby Jesus, are flanked by a headless John the Baptist and a pensive John the Evangelist. The chairs are there so you can study it. If you know the Book of Revelation, you'll understand St. John's wild and intricate vision. The St. Ursula Shrine, an ornate little mini-church in the same room, is filled with impressive detail.

○ See Memling Museum Tour.

• *Continue south (with the museum behind you, turn right) about 150 yards on Mariastraat. Turn right on Walstraat (a small black-and-white sign points the way to Minnewater and the Begijnhof). It leads into the pleasant square called Walplein, where you'll find the...*

De Halve Maan Brewery Tour

If you like beer, take a tour here (Walplein 26).

• *Leaving the brewery, head right, make your first right, and you'll see a pedestrian bridge on the right. From here, the lacy cuteness of Bruges crescendos as you approach the Begijnhof.*

Begijnhof

Begijnhofs (pronounced gutturally: buh-HHHINE-hof) were built to house women of the lay order, called Beguines, who spent their lives in piety and service without having to take the same vows a nun would. For military and other reasons, there were more women than men in the medieval Low Countries. The order of Beguines offered women (often single or widowed) a dignified place to live and work. When the order died out, many *begijnhofs* were taken over by towns for subsidized housing. Today, single religious women live in the small homes. Benedictine nuns live in a building

nearby. Tour the simple museum to get a sense of Beguine life.

In the church, the rope that dangles from the ceiling is yanked by a nun to announce a sung vespers service.

• *Exiting opposite the way you entered, you'll hook left and see a lake.*

Minnewater

Just south of the Begijnhof is Minnewater ("Water of Love"), a peaceful, lake-filled park with canals and swans. This was once far from quaint—a busy harbor where small boats shuttled cargo from the big, ocean-going ships into town. From this point, the cargo was transferred again to flat-bottomed boats that went through the town's canals to their respective warehouses and to Market Square.

When locals see these swans, they recall the 15th-century mayor—famous for his long neck—who collaborated with the Austrians. The townsfolk beheaded him as a traitor. The Austrians warned them that similarly long-necked swans would inhabit the place to forever remind them of this murder. And they do.

• *You're a five-minute walk from the train station, where you can catch a bus to Market Square, or a 15-minute walk from Market Square—take your pick.*

BRUGES CITY WALK

GROENINGE MUSEUM TOUR

In the 1400s, Bruges was northern Europe's richest, most cosmopolitan, and most cultured city. New ideas, fads, and painting techniques were imported and exported with each shipload. Beautiful paintings were soon an affordable luxury, like fancy clothes or furniture. Internationally known artists set up studios in Bruges, producing portraits and altarpieces for wealthy merchants from all over Europe.

The Groeninge Museum, understandably, has one of the world's best collections of the art produced in the city and surrounding area. This early Flemish art is less appreciated and understood today than the Italian Renaissance art produced a century later. But by selecting 11 masterpieces, we'll get an introduction to this subtle, technically advanced, and beautiful style. Hey, if you can master the museum's name (HHHROON-ih-guh), you can certainly handle the art.

ORIENTATION

Cost: €8, includes audioguide.

Hours: Tue–Sun 9:30–17:00, closed Mon.

Special Exhibit: The museum will host a special exhibit on Charles the Bold from March to July of 2009.

Getting There: The museum is at Dijver 12, near the Gruuthuse Museum and Church of Our Lady. One big copper sign and several small *museum* signs mark the nearby area, leading you to the Groeninge's modern, glass front door.

Information: Tel. 050-448-743.
Length of This Tour: Allow one hour.

Overview

The included audioguide allows you to wander as you like. Use this chapter as background to the huge collection's highlights, then browse, punching in the numbers of the paintings you'd like to learn more about.

THE TOUR BEGINS

• *In Room 1, look for...*

Gerard David (c. 1455-1523)—*Judgment of Cambyses* (1498)

That's gotta hurt.

A man is stretched across a table and skinned alive in a very businesslike manner. The crowd hardly notices, and a dog just

scratches himself. According to legend, the man was a judge arrested for corruption (left panel) and flayed (right panel), then his skin was draped (right panel background) over the new judge's throne.

Gerard David, Memling's successor as the city's leading artist, painted this for the City Hall. City councilors could ponder what might happen to them if they abused their offices.

By David's time, Bruges was in serious decline, with a failing economy and struggles against the powerful Austrian Habsburg family. The Primitive style was also fading. Italian art was popular, so David tries to spice up his retro-Primitive work with pseudo-Renaissance knickknacks—*putti* (baby angels, over the judgment throne), Roman-style medallions, and garlands. But he couldn't quite master the Italian specialty of 3-D perspective. We view the flayed man at an angle from slightly above, but the table he lies on is shown more from the side.

• *Head to Room 2 for...*

Jan van Eyck (c. 1390-1441)—*Virgin and Child with Canon Joris van der Paele* (1436)

Jan van Eyck was the world's first and greatest oil painter, and this is his masterpiece—three debatable but defensible assertions.

Mary, in a magnificent red gown, sits playing with her little baby, Jesus. Jesus glances up as St. George, the dragon-slaying

knight, enters the room, tips his cap, and says, "I'd like to introduce my namesake, George (Joris)." Mary glances down at the kneeling Joris, a church official dressed in white. Joris takes off his glasses and looks up from his prayer book to see a bishop in blue, St. Donatian, patron of the church he hopes to be buried in.

Canon Joris, who hired Van Eyck, is not a pretty sight. He's old and wrinkled, with a double chin, weird earlobes, and bloodshot eyes. But the portrait isn't unflattering, it just shows unvarnished reality with crystal clarity.

Van Eyck brings Mary and the saints down from heaven and into a typical (rich) Bruges home. He strips off their haloes, banishes all angels, and pulls the plug on heavenly radiance. If this is a religious painting, then where's God?

God's in the details. From the bishop's damask robe and Mary's wispy hair to the folds in Jesus' baby fat and the oriental carpet to "Adonai" (Lord) written on St. George's breastplate, the painting is as complex and beautiful as God's creation. The color scheme—red Mary, white canon, and blue-and-gold saints—are Bruges' city colors, from its coat of arms.

Mary, crowned with a jeweled "halo" and surrounded by beautiful things, makes an appearance in 1400s Bruges, where she can be adored in all her human beauty by Canon Joris...and by us, reflected in the mirror-like shield on St. George's back.

Jan van Eyck—*Portrait of Margareta van Eyck* (1439)

At 35, shortly after moving to Bruges, Jan van Eyck married 20-year-old Margareta. They had two kids, and after Jan died, Margareta took charge of his studio of assistants and kept it running until her death. This portrait (age 33), when paired with a matching self-portrait of Jan, was one of Europe's first husband-and-wife companion sets.

She sits half-turned, looking out of the frame. (Jan might have seen this "where-have-you-been?" expression in the window late one night.) She's dressed in a red, fur-lined coat, and we catch a glimpse of her wedding ring. Her hair is invisible—very fashionable at the time—pulled back

---

Flemish Primitives

Despite the "Primitive" label, the Low Countries of the 1400s (along with Venice and Florence) produced the most refined art in Europe. Here are some common features of Flemish Primitive art:

- **Primitive 3-D Perspective:** Expect unnaturally cramped-looking rooms, oddly slanted tables, and flat, cardboard-cutout people with stiff posture. Yes, these works are more primitive (hence the label) than those with the later Italian Renaissance perspective.
- **Realism:** Everyday bankers and clothmakers in their Sunday best are painted with clinical, warts-and-all precision. Even saints and heavenly visions are brought down to earth.
- **Details:** Like meticulous Bruges craftsmen, painters used fine-point brushes to capture almost microscopic details—flower petals, wrinkled foreheads, intricately patterned clothes, the sparkle in a ruby. The closer you get to a painting, the better it looks.
- **Oil Painted on Wood:** They were the pioneers of new-fangled oil-based paint (while Italy still used egg-yolk tempera), working on wood, before canvas became popular.
- **Portraits and Altarpieces:** Wealthy merchants and clergymen paid to have themselves painted either alone or mingling with saints.
- **Symbolism:** In earlier times, everyone understood that a dog symbolized fidelity, a lily meant chastity, and a rose was love.
- **Materialism:** Rich Flanders celebrated the beauty of luxury goods—the latest Italian dresses, jewels, carpets, oak tables—and the ordinary beauty that radiates from flesh-and-blood people.

tightly, bunched into horn-like hairnets, and draped with a head-dress. Stray hairs along the perimeter were plucked to achieve the high forehead look.

This simple portrait is revolutionary—one of history's first individual portraits that wasn't of a saint, king, duke, or pope, and wasn't part of a religious work. It signals the advent of humanism, celebrating the glory of ordinary people. Van Eyck proudly signed the work on the original frame, with his motto saying he painted it *"als ik kan" (ALC IXH KAN)...*"as good as I can."

Rogier van der Weyden (c. 1399–1464)—*St. Luke Drawing the Virgin's Portrait* (c. 1435)

Rogier van der Weyden, the other giant among the Flemish

Primitives, adds the human touch to Van Eyck's rather detached precision.

As Mary prepares to nurse, baby Jesus can't contain his glee, wiggling his fingers and toes, anticipating lunch. Mary, dressed in everyday clothes, doesn't try to hide her love as she tilts her head down with a proud smile. Meanwhile, St. Luke (the patron saint of painters, who was said to have experienced this vision) looks on intently with a sketch pad in his hand, trying to catch the scene. These small gestures, movements, and facial expressions add an element of human emotion that later artists would amplify.

The painting is neatly divided by a spacious view out the window, showing a river stretching off to a spacious horizon. Van der Weyden experimented with 3-D effects like this one (though ultimately it's just window-dressing).

Rogier van der Weyden—*Duke Philip the Good* (c. 1450)

Tall, lean, and elegant, this charismatic duke transformed Bruges from a commercial powerhouse to a cultural one. In 1425, Philip moved his court to Bruges, making it the de facto capital of a Burgundian empire stretching from Amsterdam to Switzerland.

Philip wears a big hat to hide his hair, a fashion trend he himself began. He's also wearing the gold-chain necklace of the Order of the Golden Fleece, a distinguished knightly honor he gave himself. He inaugurated the Golden Fleece in a lavish ceremony at the Bruges City Hall, complete with parades, jousting, and festive pies that contained live people hiding inside to surprise his guests.

As a lover of painting, hunting, fine clothes, and many mistresses, Philip was a role model for Italian princes, such as Lorenzo the Magnificent—the *uomo universale,* or Renaissance Man.

Hugo van der Goes (c. 1430–c. 1482)—*Death of the Virgin* (c. 1470)

The long deathwatch is over—their beloved Mary has passed on, and the disciples are bleary-eyed and dazed with grief, as though hit with a spiritual two-by-four. Each etched face is a study in sad-

Oil Paint

Take vegetable oil pressed from linseeds (flax), blend in dry powdered pigments, whip to a paste the consistency of room-temperature butter, then brush onto a panel of white-washed oak—you're painting in oils. First popularized in the early 1400s, oil eventually overshadowed egg-yolk-based tempera. Though tempera was great for making fine lines shaded with simple blocks of color, oil could blend colors together seamlessly.

Watch a master create a single dog's hair: He paints a dark stroke of brown, then lets it dry. Then comes a second layer painted over it, of translucent orange. The brown shows through, blending with the orange to match the color of a collie. Finally, he applies a third, transparent layer (a "glaze"), giving the collie her healthy sheen.

Many great artists were not necessarily great painters (e.g., Michelangelo). Van Eyck, Rembrandt, Hals, Velázquez, and Rubens were master painters, meticulously building objects with successive layers of paint...but they're not everyone's favorite artists.

ness, as they all have their own way of coping—lighting a candle, fidgeting, praying, or just staring off into space. Blues and reds dominate, and there's little eye-catching ornamentation, which lets the lined faces and expressive hand gestures do the talking.

Hugo van der Goes painted this, his last major work, the

same year he attempted suicide. Hugo had built a successful career in Ghent, then abruptly dropped out to join a monastery. His paintings became increasingly emotionally charged, and his personality more troubled.

Above the bed floats a heavenly vision, as Jesus and the angels prepare to receive Mary's soul. Their smooth skin and serene expressions contrast with the gritty, wrinkled death pallor of those on earth. Caught up in their own grief, the disciples can't see the silver lining.

• *Head to Room 3 for the surreal scene that's...*

Attributed to Hieronymus Bosch (c. 1450–1516)— *Last Judgment* (late 15th century)

It's the end of the world, and Christ descends in a bubble to pass judgment on puny humans. Little naked people dance and cavort in a theme park of medieval symbolism, desperately trying to squeeze

GROENINGE MUSEUM

in their last bit of fun. Meanwhile, some wicked souls are being punished, victims either of their own stupidity or of genetically engineered demons. The good are sent to the left panel to frolic in the innocence of paradise, while the rest are damned to hell (right panel) to be tortured under a burning sky. Bosch paints the scenes with a high horizon line, making it seem that the chaos extends forever.

The bizarre work of Bosch (who, by the way, was not from Bruges) is open to many interpretations, but some see it as a warning for the turbulent times. He painted during the dawn of a new age. Secular ideas and materialism were encroaching, and the pious and serene medieval world was shattering into chaos.

• *At the entrance to Room 4 is...*

Jan Provoost (c. 1465–1529)—*Death and the Miser*

A Bruges businessman in his office strikes a deal with Death. The grinning skeleton lays coins on the table, and in return, the man—looking unhealthy and with fear in his eyes—reaches across the

divide in the panels to give Death a promissory note, then marks the transaction in his ledger book. He's trading away a few years of his life for a little more money. The worried man on the right (the artist's self-portrait) says, "Don't do it."

Jan Provoost (also known as Provost) worked for businessmen like this. He knew their offices, full of moneybags, paperwork, and books. Bruges' materialistic capitalism was at odds with Christian poverty, and society was divided over whether to praise or condemn it. Ironically, this painting's flip side is a religious work bought and paid for by...rich merchants.

Petrus Christus (c. 1420–c. 1475)—*Annunciation and Nativity* (1452)

Italian art was soon all the rage. Ships from Genoa and Venice would unload Renaissance paintings, wowing the Northerners

No Joke

An enthusiastic American teenager approaches the ticket seller at the Groeninge Museum:
    "This is the Torture Museum, right?!"
    "No," the ticket man replies, "it's art."
    "Oh..." mumbles the kid, "art...."
    And he walks away, not realizing that, for him, the Groeninge Museum would be torture.

with their window-on-the-world, 3-D realism. Petrus Christus, one of Jan van Eyck's students, studied the Italian style and set out to conquer space.

The focus of his *Annunciation* panel is not the winged angel announcing Jesus' coming birth, nor is it the swooning, astonished Mary—it's the empty space between them. Your eye focuses back across the floor tiles and through the open doorway to gabled houses on a quiet canal in the far distance.

In the *Nativity* panel, the three angels hovering overhead really should be bigger, and the porch over the group looks a little rickety. Compared to the work of Florence's Renaissance painters, this is quite...primitive.

• *Fast-forward a few centuries (through Rooms 5–8), past paintings by no-name artists from Bruges' years of decline, to a couple of Belgium's 20th-century masters in Room 9...*

Paul Delvaux (1897-1994)—*Serenity* (1970)

Perhaps there's some vague connection between Van Eyck's medieval symbols and the Surrealist images of Paul Delvaux. Regardless, Delvaux gained fame for his nudes sleepwalking through moon-lit, video-game landscapes.

René Magritte (1898-1967)—*The Assault* (c. 1932)

Magritte had his own private reserve of symbolic images. The cloudy sky, female torso, windows, and horsebell (the ball with the slit) appear in other works as well. They're arranged here side by side as if they should mean something, but they—as well as the title—only serve to short-circuit your thoughts when you try to make sense of them. Magritte paints real objects with photographic clarity, then jumbles them together in new and provocative ways.

Scenes of Bruges

Remember that Jan van Eyck, Petrus Christus, Hans Memling, Gerard David, Jan Provoost, and possibly Rogier van der Weyden (for a few years) all lived and worked in Bruges.

In addition, many other artists included scenes of the pictur-esque city in their art, proving that it looks today much as it did way back when. Enjoy the many painted scenes of old Bruges as a slice-of-life peek into the city and its people back in its glory days.

GROENINGE MUSEUM

MEMLING MUSEUM TOUR

Located in the former hospital wards and church of St. John's Hospital, the Memling Museum (Memling in Sint-Jan Hospitaalmuseum) offers a glimpse into medieval medicine, displaying surgical instruments, documents, and visual aids as you work your way to the museum's climax: several of Hans Memling's glowing masterpieces.

ORIENTATION

Cost: €8, includes fine audioguide and free loaner folding chairs (if you'd like to sit and study the paintings).

Hours: Tue–Sun 9:30–17:00, closed Mon.

Getting There: The museum is at Mariastraat 38, across the street from the Church of Our Lady.

Information: Bruges museums tel. 050-448-711.

Length of This Tour: Allow one hour.

Overview

Hans Memling's art was the culmination of Bruges' Flemish Primitive style. His serene, soft-focus, motionless scenes capture a medieval piety that was quickly fading. The popular style made Memling (c. 1430–1494) one of Bruges' wealthiest citizens, and his work was gobbled up by visiting Italian merchants, who took it home with them, cross-pollinating European art.

The displays on medieval medicine are all on one floor of the former church, with the Memlings in a chapel at the far end.

THE TOUR BEGINS

The Church as a Hospital

Some 500 years ago, the nave of this former church was lined with beds filled with the sick and dying. Nuns served as nurses. At the far end was the high altar, which once displayed Memling's *St. John Altarpiece* (which we'll see). Bedridden patients could gaze on this peaceful, colorful vision and gain a moment's comfort from their agonies.

As the museum displays make clear, medicine of the day was well-intentioned but very crude. In many ways, this was less a hos-

pital than a hospice, helping the down-and-out make the transition from this world to the next. Religious art (displayed further along in the museum) was therapeutic, addressing the patients' mental and spiritual health. The numerous Crucifixions reminded the sufferers that Christ could feel their pain, having lived it himself.

• *Continue through the displays of religious art—past paintings that make you thankful for modern medicine. Head through the wooden archway to the black-and-white tiled room where Memling's paintings are displayed. A large triptych (three-paneled altarpiece) dominates the space.*

St. John Altarpiece (a.k.a. *The Mystical Marriage of St. Catherine,* 1474)

Sick and dying patients lay in their beds in the hospital and looked at this colorful, three-part work, which sat atop the hospital/church's high altar. The piece was dedicated to the hospital's patron saints, John the Baptist and John the Evangelist (see the inscription along the bottom frame), but Memling broadened the focus to take in a vision of heaven and the end of the world.

Central Panel: Mary, with baby Jesus on her lap, sits in a canopied chair, crowned by hovering blue angels. It's an imaginary gathering of conversing saints *(sacra conversazione),* though nobody in this meditative group is saying a word or even exchanging meaningful eye contact.

Some Memling Trademarks

- Serene symmetry, with little motion or emotion
- Serious faces that are realistic but timeless, with blemishes airbrushed out
- Eye-catching details like precious carpets, mirrors, and brocaded clothes
- Glowing colors, even lighting, no shadows
- Cityscape backgrounds

Mary is flanked by the two Johns—John the Baptist to the left, and John the Evangelist (in red) to the right. Everyone else

sits symmetrically around Mary. An organist angel to the left is matched by a book-holding acolyte to the right. St. Catherine (left, in white, red, and gold) balances St. Barbara, in green, who's absorbed in her book. Behind them, classical columns are also perfectly balanced left and right.

At the center of it all, baby Jesus tips the balance by leaning over to place a ring on Catherine's finger, sealing the "mystical marriage" between them.

St. Catherine of Alexandria, born rich, smart, and pagan to Roman parents, joined the outlawed Christian faith. She spoke out against pagan Rome, attracting the attention of the emperor, Maxentius, who sent 50 philosophers to talk some sense into her—but she countered every argument, even converting the emperor's own wife. Maxentius killed his wife, then asked Catherine to marry him. She refused, determined to remain true to the man she'd already "married" in a mystical vision—Christ.

Frustrated, Maxentius ordered Catherine to be stretched across a large, spiked wheel (the rather quaint-looking object at her feet), but the wheel flew apart, sparing her and killing many of her torturers. So they just cut her head off, which is why she has a sword, along with her "Catherine Wheel."

Looking through the columns, we see scenes of Bruges. Just to the right of the chair's canopy, the wooden contraption is a crane, used to hoist barrels from barges on Kraanplein.

Left Panel—The Beheading of John the Baptist: Even this gruesome scene, with blood still spurting from John's severed neck, becomes serene under Memling's gentle brush. Everyone is solemn, graceful, and emotionless—including both parts of the decapitated John. Memling depicts Salomé (in green) receiving the

head on her silver platter with a humble servant's downcast eyes, as if accepting her role in God's wonderful, if sometimes painful, plan.

In the background, left, we can look into Herod's palace, where he sits at a banquet table with his wife while Salomé dances modestly in front of him. Herod's lust is only hinted at with the naked statues—a man between two women—that adorn the palace exterior.

Right Panel—John the Evangelist's Vision of the Apocalypse: John sits on a high, rocky bluff on the island of Patmos and sees the end of the world as we know it...and he feels fine.

Overhead, in a rainbow bubble, God appears on his throne, resting his hand on a sealed book. A lamb steps up to open the seals, unleashing the awful events at the end of time. Standing at the bottom of the rainbow, an angel in green gestures to John and says, "Write this down." John starts to dip his quill into the inkwell (his other hand holds the quill-sharpener), but he pauses, absolutely transfixed, experiencing the Apocalypse now.

He sees wars, fires, and plagues on the horizon, the Virgin in the sky rebuking a red dragon, and many other wonders. Fervent fundamentalists should bring their Bibles along, because there are many specific references brought to life in a literal way.

In the center ride the dreaded Four Horsemen, wreaking havoc on the cosmos (galloping over either islands or clouds). Horseman number four is a skeleton, followed by a human-eating monster head. Helpless mortals on the right seek shelter in the rocks, but find none.

Memling has been criticized for building a career by copying the formulas of his predecessors, but this panel is a complete original. Its theme had never been so fully expressed, and the bright, contrasting colors and vivid imagery are almost modern. In the *St. John Altarpiece,* Memling shows us the full range of his palette, from medieval grace to Renaissance symmetry, from the real to the surreal.

• *In a glass case, find the...*

St. Ursula Shrine (c. 1489)

On October 21, 1489, the mortal remains of St. Ursula were brought here to the church and placed in this gilded oak shrine, built spe-

cially for the occasion and decorated with paintings by Memling. Ursula, yet another Christian martyred by the ancient Romans, became a sensation in the Middle Ages when builders in Germany's Köln (Cologne) unearthed a huge pile of bones believed to belong to her and her 11,000 slaughtered cohorts.

The shrine, carved of wood and covered with gold, looks like a miniature Gothic church (similar to the hospital church). Memling was asked to fill in the "church's" stained-glass windows with six arch-shaped paintings telling Ursula's well-known legend.

• *Stand in the middle of the room, facing the shrine. "Read" the shrine's story from left to right, circling counterclockwise, but begin with the...*

Left Panel: Ursula—in white and blue—arrives by boat at the city of Köln and enters through the city gate. She's on a pilgrimage to Rome, accompanied by 11,000 (female) virgins. That night (look in the two windows of the house in the background, right), an angel appears and tells her this trip will mean her death, but she is undaunted.

Center Panel: Continuing up the Rhine, they arrive in Basel. (Memling knew the Rhine, having grown up near it.) Memling condenses the 11,000 virgins to a more manageable 11, making each one pure enough for a thousand. From Basel, they set out on foot (in the background, right) over the snowy Alps.

Right Panel: They arrive in Rome—formally portrayed by a round Renaissance tower decorated with *putti* (little angels)— where Ursula falls to her knees before the pope at the church steps. Kneeling behind Ursula is her fiancé, Etherus, the pagan prince of England. She has agreed to marry him only if he becomes a Christian and refrains from the marriage bed long enough for her to make this three-year pilgrimage as a virgin (making, I guess, number 11,001). Inside the church on the right side, he is baptized a Christian.

Opposite Side—Left Panel: They head back home. Here, they're leaving Basel, boarding ships to go north on the Rhine. The pope was so inspired by these virgins that he joined them. These "crowd" scenes are hardly realistic—more like a collage of individual poses and faces. And Memling tells the story with extremely minimal acting. Perhaps his inspiration was the pomp and ceremony of Bruges parades, which were introduced by the

Burgundian dukes. He would have seen *tableaux vivants,* where Brugeois would pose in costume like human statues to enact an event from the Bible or from city history. (American "living Christmas crèches" carry on this dying art form.)

Middle Panel: Back in Köln, a surprise awaits them—the city has been taken over by vicious Huns. They grab Etherus and stab him. He dies in Ursula's arms.

Right Panel: The Hun king (in red with turban and beard) woos Ursula, placing his hand over his heart, but she says, "No

way." So a Hun soldier draws his arrow and prepares to shoot her dead. Even here, at the climax of the story, there are no histrionics. Even the dog just sits down, crosses his paws, and watches. The whole shrine cycle is as posed, motionless, and colorful as the *tableaux vivants* that may have inaugurated the shrine here in this church in 1489.

In the background behind Ursula, a Bruges couple looks on sympathetically. This may be Memling himself (in red coat with fur lining) and his wife, Anna, who bore his three children. Behind them, Memling renders an accurate city skyline of Köln, including a side view of the Köln Cathedral (missing its still-unfinished tall spires).

• *In the small adjoining room, find several more Memlings.*

Portrait of a Young Woman (1480)

Memling's bread-and-butter was portraits done for families of wealthy merchants (especially visiting Italians and Portuguese). This portrait takes us right back to that time.

The young woman looks out of the frame as if she were look-ing out a window. Her hands rest on the "sill," with the fingertips sticking over. The frame is original, but the banner and Van Eyck–like lettering are not.

Her clothes look somewhat simple, but they were high-class in their day. A dark damask dress is brightened by a red sash and a detachable white collar. She's pulled her hair into a tight bun at the back, pinned there with a fez-like cap and draped with a transparent veil. She's shaved her hairline and plucked her brows to get that clean, high-forehead look. Her ensemble is animated by a well-placed necklace of small stones.

Memling accentuates her fashionably pale complexion and gives her a pensive, sober expression, portraying her like a medieval saint. Still, she keeps her personality, with distinct features like the broad nose, neck tendons, and realistic hands. She peers out from her subtly painted veil, which sweeps down over the side of her face. What's she thinking?

Diptych of Martin van Nieuwenhove (1489)

Three-dimensional effects—borrowed from the Italian Renaissance style—enliven this traditional two-panel altarpiece. Both Mary-and-Child and the 23-year-old Martin, though in different panels, inhabit the same room within the painting.

Stand right in front of Mary, facing her directly. If you line up the paintings' horizons (seen in the distance, out the room's windows), you'll see that both panels depict the same room—a room with two windows at the back and two along the right wall.

Want proof? In the convex mirror on the back wall (just to the left of Mary), the scene is reflected back at us, showing Mary and Martin from behind, silhouetted in the two "windows" of the picture frames. Apparently, Mary makes house calls, appearing right in the living room of the young donor Martin, the wealthy, unique-looking heir to his father's business.

SLEEPING

Bruges is a great place to sleep, with Gothic spires out your window, no traffic noise, and the cheerily out-of-tune carillon heralding each new day at 8:00 sharp. (Thankfully, the bell tower is silent from 22:00 to 8:00.) Most Bruges accommodations are located between the train station and the old center, with the most distant (and best) being a few blocks to the north and east of Market Square.

B&Bs offer the best value (listed after "Hotels"). All are on quiet streets and (with a few exceptions) keep the same prices throughout the year.

Bruges is most crowded Friday and Saturday evenings from Easter through October, with July and August weekends being the worst. Many hotels charge a bit more on Friday and Saturday, and won't let you stay just one night if it's a Saturday.

Hotels
$$$ Hotel Heritage offers 24 rooms, with chandeliers that seem hung especially for you, in a solid and completely modernized old building with luxurious public spaces. Tastefully decorated and offering all the amenities, it's one of those places that does everything just right yet still feels warm and inviting—if you can afford it (Db-€192, superior Db-€238, deluxe Db-€286, includes breakfast, skipping their fine breakfast saves €17 per person, non-smoking, air-con, elevator, Internet access, sauna, tanning bed, fitness room, bike rental, Niklaas Desparsstraat 11, a block north of Market Square, tel. 050-444-444, fax 050-444-440, www.hotel-heritage.com, info@hotel-heritage.com). It's run by cheery and hardworking Johan and Isabelle Creytens.

$$$ Hotel Egmond is a creaky mansion located in the middle of the quietly idyllic Minnewater. Its eight 18th-century

Sleep Code

(€1 = about $1.40, country code: 32)
S = Single, **D** = Double/Twin, **T** = Triple, **Q** = Quad, **b** = bathroom,
s = shower only. Everyone speaks English. Unless otherwise
noted, credit cards are accepted.

To help you easily sort through these listings, I've divided
the rooms into three categories, based on the price for a
standard double room with bath:

$$$ Higher Priced—Most rooms €125 or more.
  $$ Moderately Priced—Most rooms between €80-125.
    $ Lower Priced—Most rooms €80 or less.

rooms are plain, with small modern baths shoehorned in, and the
guests-only garden is just waiting for a tea party. This hotel is ideal
for romantics who want a countryside setting—where you sleep
surrounded by a park, not a city (Sb-€97, small twin Db-€103,
larger Db-€125, Tb-€155, about €20 more Fri–Sat, parking-€10,
Minnewater 15, tel. 050-341-445, fax 050-342-940, www.egmond
.be, info@egmond.be).

$$ Hotel Adornes is small and classy—a great value situated
in the most charming part of town. This 17th-century canalside
house has 20 rooms with full modern bathrooms, free parking
(reserve in advance), free loaner bikes, and a cellar lounge with
games and videos (small Db-€120, larger Db-€140–150, Tb-€165,
Qb-€175, includes breakfast, elevator, near Carmersstraat at St.
Annarei 26, tel. 050-341-336, fax 050-342-085, www.adornes.be,
info@adornes.be). Nathalie runs the family business.

$$ Hotel Patritius, family-run and centrally located, is a
grand, circa-1830, Neoclassical mansion with hardwood oak floors
in its 16 stately rooms. It features a plush lounge, a chandeliered
breakfast room, and a courtyard garden. This is the best value in its
price range (Db-€100–122 depending on size, €10 more Fri–Sat;
Tb-€140, Qb-€165, €25 for extra bed, includes breakfast, coin-
op laundry, parking-€7, garage parking-€12, Riddersstraat 11,
tel. 050-338-454, fax 050-339-634, www.hotelpatritius.be, info
@hotelpatritius.be, Garrett and Elvi Spaey).

$$ Hotel Botaniek, quietly located a block from Astrid Park,
is a fine, pint-sized hotel with a comfy lounge, renting nine rooms
(Db-€92 weekday special for Rick Steves' readers, €98 Fri–Sat;
Tb-€120, Qb-€140, less for longer and off-season stays, free
museum-discount card, elevator, Waalsestraat 23, tel. 050-341-424,
fax 050-345-939, www.botaniek.be, info@botaniek.be, Yasmine).

$$ Hotel ter Reien is big and basic, with 26 rooms overlooking a canal in the town center (Db-€90–100, Tb-€110–130,

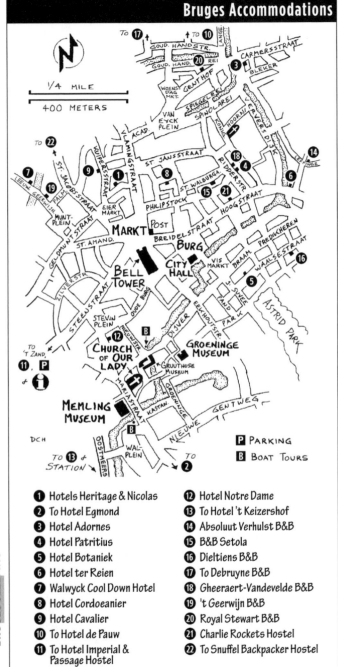

Bruges Accommodations

1 Hotels Heritage & Nicolas
2 To Hotel Egmond
3 Hotel Adornes
4 Hotel Patritius
5 Hotel Botaniek
6 Hotel ter Reien
7 Walwyck Cool Down Hotel
8 Hotel Cordoeanier
9 Hotel Cavalier
10 To Hotel de Pauw
11 To Hotel Imperial & Passage Hostel
12 Hotel Notre Dame
13 To Hotel 't Keizershof
14 Absoluut Verhulst B&B
15 B&B Setola
16 Dieltiens B&B
17 To Debruyne B&B
18 Gheeraert-Vandevelde B&B
19 't Geerwijn B&B
20 Royal Stewart B&B
21 Charlie Rockets Hostel
22 To Snuffel Backpacker Hostel

P PARKING
B BOAT TOURS

Qb-€135–150, €10 off for viewless rooms, extra bed-€20, 10 percent Rick Steves discount if you ask when you reserve and show this book at check-in, includes breakfast, Internet access and Wi-Fi, Langestraat 1, tel. 050-349-100, fax 050-340-048, www.hotel terreien.be, info@hotelterreien.be, owners Diederik and Stephanie Pille-Maes).

$$ Walwyck Cool Down Hotel—a bit of modern comfort, chic design, and English verbiage in a medieval shell—is a new, nicely located hotel with 18 spacious rooms (Db-€90, includes breakfast, Wi-Fi, Leeuwstraat 8, tel. 050-616-360, www.walwyck .com, rooms@walwyck.com).

$ Hotel Cordoeanier, a charming family-run hotel, rents 22 bright, simple, well-worn rooms on a quiet street two blocks off Market Square. It's the best cheap hotel in town (Sb-€65–75, Db-€70–85, twin Db-€80–95, Tb-€90–105, Qb-€110, Quint/b-€130, these cash-only prices valid with this book, Cordoeanierstraat 16–18, tel. 050-339-051, fax 050-346-111, www .cordoeanier.be, info@cordoeanier.be, run by Kris, Veerle, and family).

$ Hotel Cavalier, with more stairs than character, rents eight decent rooms and serves a hearty buffet breakfast in a once-royal setting (Sb-€55, Db-€65, Tb-€78, Qb-€90, two lofty "backpackers' doubles" on fourth floor-€42 or €47, includes breakfast, Kuipers-straat 25, tel. 050-330-207, fax 050-347-199, www.hotelcavalier.be, info@hotelcavalier.be, run by friendly Viviane De Clerck).

$ Hotel de Pauw is tall, skinny, and family-run, with eight straightforward rooms on a quiet street next to a church (Sb-€65, Db-€70–80, free and easy street parking, Sint Gilliskerkhof 8, tel. 050-337-118, fax 050-345-140, www.hoteldepauw.be, info @hoteldepauw.be, Philippe and Hilde).

$ Hotel Nicolas feels like an old-time boarding house that missed Bruges' affluence bandwagon. Its 14 big, plain rooms are a good value, and the location is ideal—on a quiet street a block off Market Square (Sb-€50, Db-€60–62, Tb-€73, includes breakfast, Niklaas Desparsstraat 9, tel. 050-335-502, fax 050-343-544, www .hotelnicolas.be, hotel.nicolas@telenet.be, Yi-Ling and Thomas).

$ Hotel Imperial is an old-school hotel with seven old-school rooms. It's simple and well-run in a charming building on a handy, quiet street. The fact that Paul Bernolet and Hilde don't use email fits its character (Db-€65–80, includes breakfast, Dweersstraat 24, tel. 050-339-014, fax 050-344-306).

$ Hotel Notre Dame is a humble and blocky little budget option, renting 12 decent rooms in the busy thick of things (Db-€70–75, includes breakfast, Mariastraat 3, tel. 050-333-193, fax 050-337-608, www.hotelnotredame.be, info@hotelnotredame.be).

Near the Train Station: **$ Hotel 't Keizershof** is a dollhouse of a hotel that lives by its motto, "Spend a night...not a fortune." It's simple and tidy, with seven small, cheery, old-time rooms split between two floors, with a shower and toilet on each (S-€25, D-€44, T-€66, Q-€80, includes breakfast, cash only, free and easy parking, laundry service-€7.50, Oostmeers 126, a block in front of station, tel. 050-338-728, www.hotelkeizershof.be, info @hotelkeizershof.be). The hotel is run by Stefaan and Hilde, with decor by their children, Lorie and Fien.

Bed-and-Breakfasts

These B&Bs, run by people who enjoy their work, offer a better value than hotels. Most families rent out their entire top floor—generally three rooms and a small sitting area. And most are mod and stylish, they're just in medieval shells. Each is central, with lots of stairs and €70 doubles you'd pay €100 for in a hotel. Most places charge €10 extra for one-night stays. It's possible to find parking on the street in the evening (pay 9:00–19:00, 2-hour maximum for metered parking during the day, free overnight).

$$ Absoluut Verhulst is a great, modern-feeling B&B in a 400-year-old house, run by friendly Frieda and Benno (Db-€90, huge and lofty suite-€120 for two, €140 for three, and €160 for four, €10 more for one-night stays, cash only, non-smoking, Wi-Fi, five-minute walk east of Market Square at Verbrand Nieuwland 1, tel. 050-334-515, www.b-bverhulst.com, b-b.verhulst@pandora.be).

$ B&B Setola, run by Lut and Bruno Setola, offers three modern expansive rooms and a spacious breakfast/living room on the top floor of their house. The family room has a fun loft (Sb-€60, Db-€70, €20 per extra person, €10 more for one-night stays, Wi-Fi, 5-min walk from Market Square, Sint Walburgastraat 12, tel. 050-334-977, fax 050-332-551, www.bedandbreakfast-bruges .com, setola@bedandbreakfast-bruges.com).

$ Koen and Annemie Dieltiens are a friendly couple who enjoy getting to know their guests while sharing a wealth of information on Bruges. You'll eat a hearty breakfast around a big table in their comfortable house (Sb-€60, Db-€70, Tb-€90, €10 more for one-night stays, cash only, Wi-Fi, Waalse Straat 40, three blocks southeast of Burg Square, tel. 050-334-294, www.bedand breakfastbruges.be, dieltiens@bedandbreakfastbruges.be).

$ Debruyne B&B, run by Marie-Rose and her architect husband, Ronny, offers three rooms with artsy, original decor (check out the elephant-size white doors—Ronny's design) and genuine warmth. If Gothic is getting old, this is refreshingly modern (Sb-€55, Db-€60, Tb-€90, €10 more for one-night stays, cash only, Internet access, seven-minute walk north of Market Square, two blocks from the little church at Lange Raamstraat 18, tel. 050-347-

606, www.bedandbreakfastbruges.com, mietjedebruyne@yahoo
.co.uk).

$ Paul and Roos Gheeraert-Vandevelde live in a Neoclassical
mansion and rent three huge, bright, comfy rooms (Sb-€60,
Db-€70, Tb-€90, two-night minimum stay required, cash only,
strictly non-smoking, fridges in rooms, Internet access and Wi-Fi,
Riddersstraat 9, 5-min walk east of Market Square, tel. 050-335-
627, fax 050-345-201, www.bb-bruges.be, bb-bruges@skynet.be).

$ 't Geerwijn B&B, run by Chris de Loof, offers homey
rooms in the old center. Check out the fun, lofty A-frame room
upstairs (Ds/Db-€65, Tb-€75, pleasant breakfast room and a royal
lounge, cash only, non-smoking, Geerwijnstraat 14, tel. 050-340-
544, fax 050-343-721, www.geerwijn.be, chris.deloof@scarlet.be).
Chris also rents an apartment that sleeps five (€100).

$ Royal Stewart B&B, run by Scottish Maggie and her
husband, Gilbert, has three thoughtfully decorated rooms in a
quiet, almost cloistered 17th-century house that was inhabited by
nuns until 1953 (S-€45, D/Db-€62, Tb-€82, cash only, pleasant
breakfast room, Genthof 25–27, 5-min walk from Market Square,
tel. 050-337-918, fax 050-337-918, www.royalstewart.be, r.stewart
@pandora.be).

Hostels
Bruges has several good hostels offering beds for around €15
in two- to eight-bed rooms. Breakfast is about €3 extra. The
American-style **$ Charlie Rockets** hostel (and bar) is the liveliest
and most central. The ground floor feels like a 19th-century sports
bar, with a foosball-and-movie-posters party ambience. Upstairs is
an industrial-strength pile of hostel dorms (90 beds, €16 per bed
with sheets, 4–6 beds per room, D-€50, lockers, Hoogstraat 19,
tel. 050-330-660, www.charlierockets.com). Other small, loose,
and central places are **$ Snuffel Backpacker Hostel** (56 beds,
€14–18 per bed includes sheets and breakfast, 4–14 beds per room,
open 24/7, Ezelstraat 47, tel. 050-333-133, www.snuffel.be) and the
minimal and funky **$ Passage** (€14, 4–7 beds per room, D-€50,
Db-€65, prices include sheets, Dweerstraat 26, tel. 050-340-232,
www.passagebruges.com, info@passagebruges.com).

EATING AND NIGHTLIFE

Belgium is where France meets northern Europe, and you'll find a good mix of both Flemish and French influences in Bruges and Brussels. As you're enjoying Belgian cuisine, it's interesting to note that the Flemish were ruled by the French and absorbed some of the fancy cuisine and etiquette of their overlords. The Dutch, on the other hand, were ruled by the Spanish for 80 years and picked up nothing.

Popular Throughout Belgium

Moules: Mussels are served everywhere, either cooked plain *(nature)*, with white wine *(vin blanc)*, with shallots or onions *(marinière)*, or in a tomato sauce *(provençale)*. You get a big-enough-for-two bucket and a pile of fries. Go local by using one empty shell to tweeze out the rest of the *moules.* When the mollusks are in season, from about mid-July through April, you'll get the big Dutch mussels. Locals take a break in May and June, when only the puny Danish kind are available.

Frites: Belgian-style fries *(Vlaamse frites,* or Flemish fries) taste so good because they're deep-fried twice—once to cook, and once to brown. The natives eat them with mayonnaise, not ketchup.

Flemish Specialties

These specialties are traditional to Bruges, but also available in Brussels.

Carbonnade: Rich beef stew flavored with onions and beer.

Chou rouge à la flamande: Red cabbage with onions and prunes.

Flamiche: Cheese pie with onions.

Flemish asparagus: White asparagus (fresh in springtime) in cream sauce.

Lapin à la flamande: Marinated rabbit braised in onions and prunes.

Soupe à la bière: Beer soup.

Stoemp: Mashed potatoes and vegetables.

Waterzooi: Creamy meat stew (chicken, eel, or fish).

...à la flamande: Anything cooked in the local Flemish style.

Brussels Specialties

These specialties are "native" to Brussels (which tends toward French cuisine), but you'll find them in Bruges, too.

Anguilles au vert: Eel in green herb sauce.

Caricoles: Sea snails. Very local, seasonal, and hard to find, these are usually sold hot by street vendors.

Cheeses: Remoudou and Djotte de Nivelles are made locally.

Choux de Bruxelles: Brussels sprouts (in cream sauce).

Crevettes: Shrimp, often served as croquettes (minced and stuffed in breaded, deep-fried rolls).

Croque monsieur: Grilled ham-and-cheese sandwich.

Endive: Typical Belgian vegetable (also called *chicoree* or *chicon*) served as a side dish.

Filet américain: Beware—for some reason, steak tartare (raw) is called "American."

Tartine de fromage blanc: Open-face cream-cheese sandwich, often enjoyed with a cherry Kriek beer.

...à la brabançonne: Anything cooked in the local Brabant (Brussels) style, such as *faisant* (pheasant) *à la brabançonne.*

Desserts and Snacks

Cramique: Currant roll.

Craquelin: Currant roll with sugar sprinkles.

Dame blanche: Hot-fudge sundae.

Gaufres: Waffles, sold hot in small shops.

Pistolets: Round croissants.

Pralines: Filled Belgian chocolates.

Spekuloos: Spicy gingerbread biscuits served with coffee.

Belgian Beers

Belgium has about 120 different varieties of beer and 580 different brands, more than any other country...and the locals take their beers as seriously as the French do their wines. Even small café menus include six to eight varieties. Connoisseurs and novices alike can be confused by the many choices, and casual drinkers probably won't like every kind offered, since some varieties don't even taste like beer. Belgian beer is generally yeastier and higher in alcohol than beers in other countries.

In Belgium, certain beers are paired with certain dishes. To bring out their flavor, different beers are served at cold, cool, or room temperature, and each has its own distinctive glass. Whether wide-mouthed, tall, or fluted, with or without a stem, the glass is meant to highlight the beer's qualities. A memorable Belgian beer experience is drinking a Kwak beer in its traditional tall glass. The glass, which widens at the base, stands in a wooden holder, and you pick the whole apparatus up—frame and glass—and drink. As you near the end, the beer in the wide bottom comes out at you quickly, with a "Kwak! Kwak! Kwak!" Critics say this gimmick distracts from the fact that Kwak beer is mediocre at best.

To get a draft beer in Bruges, where Flemish is the dominant language, ask for *een pintje* (ayn pinch-ya; a pint), and in Brussels, where French prevails, request *une bière* (oon bee-yair). Don't insist on beer from the tap. The only way to offer so many excellent beers fresh is to serve them bottled, and the best varieties are generally available only by the bottle. "Cheers" is *proost* or *gezondheid* in Flemish, and *santé* (sahn-tay) in French. The colorful cardboard coasters make nice, free souvenirs.

Here's a breakdown of types of beer, with some common brand names you'll find either on tap or in bottles. (Some beers require a second fermentation in the bottle, so they're only available in bottles.) This list is just a start, and you'll find many beers that don't fall into these neat categories. For encyclopedic information on Belgian beers, visit www.belgianstyle.com.

Ales (Blonde/Red/Amber/Brown): Ales are easily recognized by their color. Try a blonde or golden ale (Leffe Blonde, Duvel), a rare and bitter sour red (Rodenbach), an amber (Palm, De Koninck), or a brown (Leffe Bruin). The last surviving Bruges beer is the prize-winning Brugse Zot (Bruges Fool), a golden ale.

Lagers: These are the light, sparkling, Budweiser-type beers. Popular brands include Jupiler, Stella Artois, and Maes.

Lambics: Perhaps the most unusual and least beer-like, *lambics* are stored for years in wooden casks, fermenting from wild yeasts that occur naturally in the air. Tasting more like a dry and bitter farmhouse cider, pure *lambic* is often blended with fruits to counter the sour flavor. Some brand names include Cantillon, Lindemans, and Mort-Subite ("Sudden Death").

Fruit *lambics* include those made with cherries *(kriek)*, raspberries *(frambozen)*, peaches *(pêche)*, or black currants *(cassis)*. The result for each is a tart but sweet beer, similar to a dry pink champagne. People who don't usually enjoy beer tend to like these fruit-flavored varieties.

White *(Witte)*: Based on wheat instead of hops, these are milky-yellow summertime beers. White beer, similar to a Hefeweizen in the United States, is often flavored with spices such as orange peel or coriander.

Trappist Beers: For centuries, between their vespers and matins, Trappist monks have been brewing heavily fermented, malty beers. Three typical Trappist beers (from the Westmalle monastery) are Trippel, with a blonde color, served cold with a frothy head; Dubbel, which is dark, sweet, and served cool; and Single, made especially by the monks for the monks, and considered a fair trade for a life of celibacy. Other Trappist monasteries include Rochefort, Chimay, and Orval. Try the Trappist Blauwe Chimay—extremely smooth, milkshake-like, and complex.

Strong Beers: The potent brands include Duvel (meaning "devil," because of its high octane, camouflaged by a pale color), Verboten Vrucht ("forbidden fruit," with Adam and Eve on the label), and the not-for-the-fainthearted brands of Judas, Satan, and Lucifer. Gouden Carolus is good and Delerium Tremens speaks for itself.

Mass-Produced Beers: Connoisseurs say you should avoid the mass-produced labels (Leffe, Stella, and Hoegaarden—all owned by InBev, which just bought Budweiser in America) when you can enjoy a Belgian microbrew (like Chimay) instead.

RESTAURANTS

Bruges' specialties include mussels cooked a variety of ways (one order can feed two), fish dishes, grilled meats, and french fries. Don't eat before 19:30 unless you like eating alone (or with other tourists).

Tax and service are always included in your bill (though a 5–10 percent tip is appreciated). You can't get free tap water; Belgian restaurateurs are emphatic about that. While tap water comes with a smile in Holland, France, and Germany, it's not the case in Belgium, where you'll either pay for water, enjoy the beer, or go thirsty.

You'll find plenty of affordable, touristy restaurants on floodlit squares and along dreamy canals. Bruges feeds 3.5 million tourists a year, and most are seduced by a high-profile location. These can be fine experiences for the magical setting and views, but the quality of food and service will likely be low. I wouldn't blame you for eating at one of these places, but I won't recommend any. I prefer the candle-cool bistros that flicker on back streets. Here are my favorites:

Rock Fort is a chic, eight-table spot with a modern, fresh coziness and a high-powered respect for good food. Two young chefs, Peter Laloo and Hermes Vanliefde, give their French

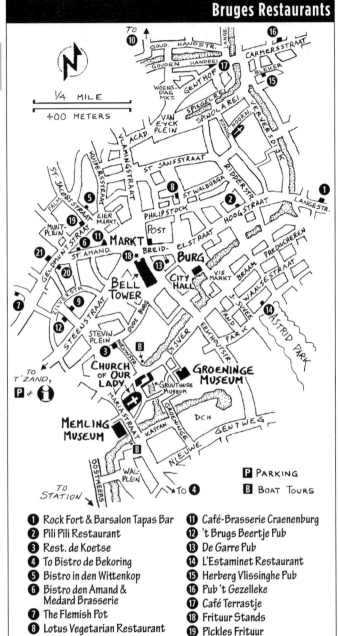

Bruges Restaurants

1. Rock Fort & Barsalon Tapas Bar
2. Pili Pili Restaurant
3. Rest. de Koetse
4. To Bistro de Bekoring
5. Bistro in den Wittenkop
6. Bistro den Amand & Medard Brasserie
7. The Flemish Pot
8. Lotus Vegetarian Restaurant
9. The Hobbit
10. To Tom's Diner
11. Café-Brasserie Craenenburg
12. 't Brugs Beertje Pub
13. De Garre Pub
14. L'Estaminet Restaurant
15. Herberg Vlissinghe Pub
16. Pub 't Gezelleke
17. Café Terrastje
18. Frituur Stands
19. Pickles Frituur
20. Laurenzino Waffles
21. Gelateria Da Vinci & Grocery

cuisine a creative and gourmet twist. Reservations are required for dinner but not lunch. This place is a winner (€13 Mon–Fri lunch special with coffee, beautifully presented €19–24 dinner plates, fancy €49 fixed-price meal includes dessert, open Mon–Fri 12:00–14:30 & 18:30–23:00, closed Sat–Sun, great pastas and salads, Langestraat 15, tel. 050-334-113). They also run the Barsalon restaurant next door.

Barsalon Tapas Bar, more than a tapas bar, is the brainchild of Peter Laloo from Rock Fort (listed above), allowing him to spread his creative cooking energy. This long, skinny slice of L.A. thrives late into the evening with Bruges' beautiful people. Choose between the long bar, comfy stools, and bigger tables in back. Come early for fewer crowds. The playful menu comes with €6–10 "tapas" dishes taking you from Spain to Japan (three fill two hungry travelers) and more elaborate €14 plates. And don't overlook their daily "suggestions" board with some special wines by the glass and a "teaser" sampler plate of desserts. The €35 five-tapas special is a whole meal. Barsalon shares the same kitchen, hours, and dressy local clientele as the adjacent Rock Fort.

Pili Pili is a mod and inviting pasta eatery, where Gianna Santy handles the customers while husband Allan Hilverson prepares and serves pastas and great salads at good prices. It's clean, low-key, and brimming with quality food and snappy service (€10 lunch plate with wine, €8–10 pasta, Thu–Tue 12:00–14:30 & 18:00–22:30, closed Wed, Hoogstraat 17, tel. 050-491-149).

Restaurant de Koetse is a good bet for central, affordable, quality, local-style food. The feeling is traditional, a bit formal, and dressy yet accessible. The cuisine is Belgian and French, with an emphasis on grilled meat, seafood, and mussels (€28–37 three-course meals, €20–25 plates include vegetables and a salad, Fri–Wed 12:00–14:30 & 18:00–22:00, closed Thu, non-smoking section, Oude Burg 31, tel. 050-337-680, Piet).

Bistro de Bekoring, cute, candlelit, and Gothic, fills two almshouses and a delightful terrace with people thankful for good food. Rotund and friendly Chef Roland and his wife, Gerda, love to tempt the hungry—as the name of their bistro implies. They serve traditional Flemish food (especially eel and beer-soaked stew) from a small menu to people who like holding hands as they dine. Reservations are smart (€12 weekday lunch, €35 fixed-price dinners, €42 with wine, Wed–Sat 12:00–13:30 and from 18:30, closed Sun evening and Mon–Tue; out past the Begijnhof at Arsenaalstraat 53, tel. 050-344-157).

Bistro in den Wittenkop, very Flemish, is a stylishly cluttered, laid-back, old-time place specializing in the local favorites. While Lieve cooks, her husband Daniel serves in a cool-and-jazzy, candlelit ambience (€35 three-course meal, €20–25 plates, Tue–Sat

12:00–14:00 & 18:00–21:30, closed Sun–Mon, reserve ahead, terrace in back in summer, Sint Jakobsstraat 14, tel. 050-332-059).

Bistro den Amand, with a plain interior and a few outdoor tables, exudes unpretentious quality the moment you step in. In this mussels-free zone, Chef Arnout is enthusiastic about vegetables as his busy wok and fun salads prove. It's on a busy pedestrian lane a half-block off the Market Square (€30 three-course meal, €20 plates; Mon–Tue and Thu–Sat 12:00–14:00 & 18:00–21:00, closed Wed and Sun; Sint-Amandstraat 4, tel. 050-340-122, An Vissers and Arnout Beyaert). Reservations are smart for dinner.

The Flemish Pot (a.k.a. The Little Pancake House) is a hard-working eatery serving up traditional peasant-style meals. They crank out pancakes (savory and sweet) and homemade *wafels* for lunch. Then, at 18:00, enthusiastic chefs Mario and Rik stow their waffle irons and pull out a traditional menu of vintage Flemish specialties served in little iron pots and skillets. Seating is tight and cluttered. You'll enjoy huge portions, refills from the hovering "fries maiden," and a good selection of local beers (€26–30 three-course meals, €16–24 plates, Wed–Sun 12:00–22:00, closed Mon–Tue, reservations smart, family-friendly, just off Geldmuntstraat at Helmstraat 3, tel. 050-340-086).

Lotus Vegetarian Restaurant serves serious lunch plates (€10 *plat du jour* offered daily), salads, and homemade chocolate cake in a bustling and upscale setting without a trace of tie-dye. To keep carnivorous spouses happy, they also serve several very good, politically correct (a.k.a. organic) meat dishes (Mon–Sat from 11:45, last orders at 14:00, closed Sun, cash only, just off north of Burg Square at Wapenmakersstraat 5, tel. 050-331-078).

The Hobbit, featuring an entertaining menu, is always busy with happy eaters. For a swinging deal, try the all-you-can-eat spareribs with bread and salad for €16.50. It's nothing fancy, just good, basic food in a fun, traditional grill house (daily 18:00–24:00, family-friendly, Kemelstraat 8–10, reservations smart, tel. 050-335-520).

Tom's Diner is a trendy, stark little "bistro eetcafé" in a quiet, cobbled residential area a 10-minute walk from the center. Young chef Tom gives traditional dishes a delightful modern twist. If you want to flee the tourists and experience a popular neighborhood joint, this is it—the locals love it (€17 plates, Thu–Tue 18:00–24:00, closed Wed, north of Market Square near Sint-Gilliskerk at West-Gistelhof 23, tel. 050-333-382).

Market Square Restaurants: Most tourists seem to be eating on Market Square with the bell tower high overhead and horse carriages clip-clopping by. The square is ringed by tourist traps with aggressive waiters expert at getting you to consume more than you intended. Still, if you order smartly, you can have a memorable meal or drink here on one of the finest squares in Europe at a reasonable price. Consider **Café-Brasserie Craenenburg,** with a straightforward menu, where you can get pasta and beer for €14 and spend all the time you want ogling the magic of Bruges (daily 7:30–24:00, Markt 16, tel. 050-333-402).

Cheap Eats: **Medard Brasserie,** just a block off Market Square, serves the cheapest hot meal in town—hearty meat spaghetti (big plate-€3, huge plate-€5.50, sit inside or out, daily 11:00–20:30, Sint Amandstraat 18, tel. 050-348-684).

Bars Offering Light Meals, Beer, and Ambience

My best budget-eating tip for Bruges: Stop into one of the city's atmospheric bars for a simple meal and a couple of world-class beers with great Bruges ambience. The last three pubs listed are in the wonderfully cozy *(gezellig)* quarter, northeast of Market Square.

The **'t Brugs Beertje** is young, convivial, and smoky. While any pub or restaurant carries the basic beers, you'll find a selection here of more than 300 types, including brews to suit any season. They serve light meals, including pâté, spaghetti, toasted sandwiches, and a traditional cheese plate. You're welcome to sit at the bar and talk with the staff (five cheeses, bread, and salad for €11; Thu–Tue 16:00–24:00, closed Wed, Kemelstraat 5, tel. 050-339-616, run by fun-loving manager Daisy).

De Garre is another good place to gain an appreciation of the Belgian beer culture. Rather than a noisy pub scene, it has a dressy, sit-down-and-focus-on-your-friend-and-the-fine-beer vibe. It's mature and cozy with tables, light meals (cold cuts, pâtés, and toasted sandwiches), and a selection of 150 beers (daily 12:00–24:00, additional seating up tiny staircase, off Breidelstraat between Burg and Markt, on tiny Garre alley, tel. 050-341-029).

L'Estaminet is a youthful, jazz-filled eatery, similar to one of Amsterdam's brown cafés. Don't be intimidated by its lack of tourists. Local students flock here for the Tolkien-chic ambience, hearty €9 spaghetti, and big dinner salads. Since this is Belgium, it serves more beer than wine. For outdoor dining under an all-weather canopy, enjoy the relaxed patio facing peaceful Astrid Park (Tue–Wed and Fri–Sun 11:30–24:00, Thu 16:00–24:00, closed Mon, Park 5, tel. 050-330-916).

Herberg Vlissinghe is the oldest pub in town (1515). Bruno keeps things simple and laid-back, serving simple plates (lasagna, grilled cheese sandwiches, and famous €8 angel-hair spaghetti) and great beer in the best old-time tavern atmosphere in town. This must have been the Dutch Masters' rec room. The garden outside comes with a *boules* court—free for guests to watch or play (Wed–Sat 11:00–24:00, Sun 11:00–19:00, closed Mon–Tue, Blekersstraat 2, tel. 050-343-737).

Pub 't Gezelleke lacks the mystique of the Vlissinghe, but it's a true neighborhood pub offering small, forgettable plates and a fine chance to drink with locals. Its name is an appropriate play on the word for cozy and the name of a great local poet (Mon–Fri 11:00–24:00, closed Sat–Sun, Carmersstraat 15, tel. 050-338-381, Peter and Gried).

Café Terrastje is a cozy pub serving light meals. Experience the grown-up ambience inside, or relax on the front terrace overlooking the canal and heart of the *gezellig* district (food served 12:00–21:00, open until 23:30, closed Thu, corner of Genthof and Langerei, tel. 050-330-919, Ian and Patricia).

Fries, Fast Food, and Picnics

Local french fries *(frites)* are a treat. Proud and traditional *frituurs* serve tubs of fries and various local-style shish kebabs. Belgians dip their *frites* in mayonnaise, but ketchup is there for the Yankees (along with spicier sauces). For a quick, cheap, hot, and scenic snack, hit a *frituur* and sit on the steps or benches overlooking Market Square (convenience benches are about 50 yards past the post office).

Market Square Frituur: Twin, take-away french fry carts are on Market Square at the base of the bell tower (daily 10:00–24:00). Skip the ketchup and have a sauce adventure. I find the cart on the left more user-friendly.

Pickles Frituur, a block off Market Square, is handy for sit-down fries. Its forte is greasy, fast, deep-fried Flemish fast food. The "menu 2" comes with three traditional gut bombs: shrimp, chicken, and "spicy gypsy" sausage (daily 11:30–24:00, at the corner of Geldmuntstraat and Sint Jakobstraat, tel. 050-337-957).

Delhaize-Proxy Supermarket is ideal for picnics. Its push-button produce pricer lets you buy as few as one mushroom (Mon–Sat 9:00–19:00, closed Sun, 3 blocks off Market Square on Geldmuntstraat). For midnight snacks, you'll find Indian-run corner grocery stores scattered around town.

Belgian Waffles and Ice Cream

While Americans think of "Belgian" waffles for breakfast, the Belgians (who don't eat waffles or pancakes for breakfast) think of *wafels* as Liège-style (dense, sweet, heated up, and eaten plain) and Brussels-style (lighter, often with powdered sugar or whipped cream and strawberries, served in teahouses only in the afternoons 14:00–18:00).

You'll see waffles sold at restaurants and take-away stands. **Laurenzino** is a favorite with Bruges' teens when they get the waffle munchies. Their classic waffle with chocolate costs €2.50 (daily 10:00–23:00, across from Gelateria Da Vinci at Noordzandstraat 1, tel. 050-345-854).

Gelateria Da Vinci, the local favorite for homemade ice cream, has creative flavors and a lively atmosphere. As you approach, you'll see a line of happy lickers. Before ordering, ask to sample the Ferrero Rocher (chocolate, nuts, and crunchy cookie) and plain yogurt (daily 10:00–24:00, Geldmuntstraat 34, run by Sylvia from Austria).

NIGHTLIFE

Herberg Vlissinghe and **De Garre** are great places to just nurse a beer and enjoy new friends.

Charlie Rockets is an American-style bar—lively and central—with foosball games, darts, and five pool tables (€9/hr) in the inviting back room. It also runs a youth hostel upstairs and therefore is filled with a young, international crowd (a block off Market Square at Hoogstraat 19). It's open nightly until 3:00 in the morning with non-stop rock 'n' roll.

Nighttime Bike Ride: Great as these pubs are, my favorite way to spend a late-summer evening in Bruges is in the twilight on a rental bike, savoring the cobbled wonders of its back streets, far from the touristic commotion.

Evening Carillon Concerts: The tiny courtyard behind the bell tower has a few benches where people can enjoy the free carillon concerts (generally Mon, Wed, and Sat at 21:00 in the summer; schedule posted on the wall).

BRUSSELS
Bruxelles

ORIENTATION

Six hundred years ago, Brussels was just a nice place to stop and buy a waffle on the way to Bruges. With no strategic importance, it was allowed to grow as a free trading town. Today, it's a city of 1.8 million, the capital of Belgium, the headquarters of NATO, and the center of the European Union.

The Bruxelloise are cultured and genteel—even a bit snobby. As the unofficial capital of Europe, the city is multicultural, hosting politicians and businessmen from around the globe and featuring a world of ethnic restaurants.

Brussels enjoyed a Golden Age of peace and prosperity (1400–1550) while England and France were duking it out in the Hundred Years' War. It was then that many of the fine structures that distinguish the city today were built. In the 1800s, Brussels had another growth spurt, fueled by industrialization, wealth taken from the Belgian Congo, and the exhilaration of the country's recent independence (1830).

Brussels speaks French. Bone up on *bonjour* and *s'il vous plaît* (see the French Survival Phrases in the appendix). Though the city (and country) is officially bilingual and filled with foreign visitors, 80 percent of the locals speak French first and English second, if at all. Language aside, the whole feel of the town is urban French, not rural Flemish.

Because Brussels sits smack-dab between Belgium's two linguistic groups (60 percent of Belgians speak Flemish, 40 percent speak French), most of Brussels' street signs and maps are in both languages. In this chapter, French names are generally used.

Tourists zipping between Amsterdam and Paris by train usually miss Brussels, but its rich, chocolaty mix of food and culture pleasantly surprises those who stop.

Brussels in Three Hours

Brussels makes a great stopover between trains. First check your bag at the Central Station and confirm your departure time and station (factoring in any necessary transit time to a different departure station) before heading into town. Then do this Brussels blitz:

Head directly for the Grand Place and take my Grand Place Walk. To streamline, skip the *Manneken-Pis* until later, and end the walk at the Bourse, where you'll catch bus #95 to Place Royale. Enjoy a handful of masterpieces at the Royal Museums of Fine Arts, then do the Upper Town Walk, which ends back at the *Manneken-Pis* and the Grand Place. Buy a box of chocolates and a bottle of Belgian beer, and pop the top as your train pulls out of the station. Ahhh!

Planning Your Time

Brussels is low on great sights and high on ambience. On a quick trip, a day and a night are enough for a good first taste. It could even be done as a day trip by train from Bruges (2/hr, 1 hr) or a stopover on the Amsterdam–Paris or Amsterdam–Bruges ride (hourly trains); for specifics, see the "Brussels in Three Hours" sidebar. The main reason to stop—the Grand Place—takes only a few minutes to see. With very limited time, skip the indoor sights and enjoy a coffee or a beer on the square.

Art lovers and novices alike can spend a couple of enjoyable hours at the Royal Museums of Fine Arts of Belgium (twin museums—ancient and modern—covered by the same ticket, and a new Magritte Museum), would-be Walloons can bone up on their Belgian history at the BELvue Museum, and even the tone-deaf can appreciate the Musical Instruments Museum. To see the impressive auto and military museums (side by side), plan on a three-hour excursion from the town center.

OVERVIEW

Central Brussels is surrounded by a ring of roads (which replaced the old city wall) called the Pentagon. (Romantics think it looks more like a heart.) All hotels and nearly all the sights I mention are within this ring. The epicenter holds the main square (the Grand Place), the TI, and Central Station (all within three blocks of each other).

What isn't so apparent from maps is that Brussels is a city divided by altitude. A ridgeline that runs north–south splits the town into the Upper Town (east half, elevation 200 feet) and Lower

BRUSSELS ORIENTATION

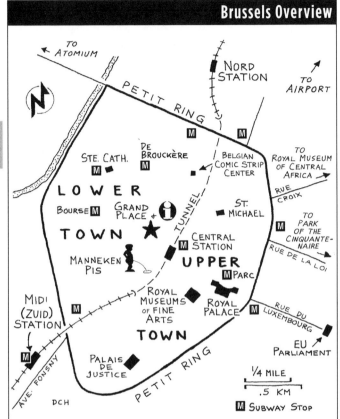

Town (west, at sea level), with the Central Station in between. The Upper Town, traditionally the home of nobility and the rich, has big marble palaces, broad boulevards, and the major museums. The Lower Town, with the Grand Place (Grote Markt in Flemish), narrow streets, old buildings, modern shops, colorful eateries, and the famous peeing-boy statue, has more character.

Outside the Pentagon-shaped center, sprawling suburbs and vast green zones contain some tourist attractions, including the European Parliament and the Park of the Cinquantenaire, along with Autoworld, the Royal Museum of the Army and Military History, and the Atomium.

Tourist Information

The TI at Rue du Marché-aux-Herbes 63 covers Brussels and Flanders, with a fine room-recommendation service (Mon–Sat 9:00–18:00, until 19:00 July–Aug, until 17:00 in winter; Sun 10:00–

17:00 year-round; three blocks downhill from Central Station, tel. 02-504-0390, www.brusselsinternational.be and www.visit flanders.com, fun Europe store nearby). There's another TI in the Town Hall on the Grand Place (summer daily 9:00–18:00, winter daily 10:00–14:00 except closed Sun Jan–Easter, tel. 02-513-8940).

The TIs have countless fliers. Day-trippers should pick up a free city map and a public transit map. The €4 *Brussels Guide & Map* booklet is worthwhile if you want a series of neighborhood walks (the Grand Place, plus three others farther afield), a map of greater Brussels, and a more complete explanation of the city's many museums. For current listings of concerts and other entertainment options, pick up the €3.50 *Bulletin* magazine, which has the monthly "What's On" inside. The **Brussels Card,** sold at the TIs, provides unlimited public transportation and free entrance to nearly all the major museums; it's worthwhile only if you plan to sightsee like mad (€20/24 hours, €28/48 hours, €33/72 hours, also sold at museums, public transportation offices, and some hotels, www.brusselsinternational.be).

Arrival in Brussels

By Train: Brussels can't decide which of its three stations (Central, Nord, and Midi) is the main one. Most international trains use the Nord and Midi stations. The Eurostar leaves from the Midi Station (also called Zuid, or South), getting you to London in less than three hours. The area around the Midi Station is a rough-and-tumble immigrant neighborhood (marked by its towering Ferris wheel); the area around the Nord Station is a seedy red light district. The Central Station, nearest to the sights and my recommended hotels, has handy services: a small grocery store, fast food, waiting rooms, and luggage storage (€4/bag—look for the *consigne* sign near track 1; or store two bags in a locker around the corner for half the price). Normally, only Belgian and Amsterdam trains stop at Central. Don't assume your train stops at more than one station; ask your conductor.

If you arrive at Nord or Midi, take a connecting train to the Central Station. Trains zip under the city, connecting all three stations every two minutes or so. It's an easy three-minute chore to connect from Nord or Midi to Central. The €1.50 ticket between the stations is covered by any train ticket into or out of Brussels (or use your railpass). Scan the departures board for trains leaving in the next few minutes and note which ones stop at Central. As you wait on the platform for your train, watch the track notice board that tells which train is approaching. They zip in and out constantly—so a train with an open door on your train's track—three minutes before your departure time—may well be the wrong train. Anxious travelers, who think their train has arrived early, often board the wrong train on the right track.

To get to the Grand Place from Central Station, exit the station from the top floor (to the left of the ticket windows), and you'll see Le Meridien Hôtel across the street. Pass through the arch of Le Meridien Hôtel, turn right, and walk downhill one block to a small square with a fountain. For the Grand Place, turn left at the far end of the square. Or, to head directly to the TI, exit the small square at the far end and continue straight for one block to Rue du Marché-aux-Herbes 63. Note that the hop-on, hop-off bus companies depart from just in front of the Central Station (you'll meet ticket hustlers as you leave). You could hop on one of these buses upon arrival to orient yourself from the top deck.

By Plane: See the Transportation Connections chapter.

Helpful Hints

Theft Alert: While I euphemistically describe Brussels as "earthy," it's also undeniably seedier than many European cities. Expect more grime on buildings, street people, and Gypsy ladies cradling their babies with a fake arm (while their hidden, real arm rifles your pockets). Muggings do occur. Some locals warn that it's not safe to be out late, especially after the Métro shuts down at midnight; troublemakers prey on people who missed that last ride. As in any other big city, use common sense and consider taking a taxi back to your hotel late at night.

Sightseeing Schedules: Brussels' most important museums are closed on Monday. But, of course, the city's single best sight—the Grand Place—is always open. You can also enjoy a bus tour any day of the week, or visit the more far-flung sights (which *are* open on Monday), such as the Atomium and the European Parliament. Most important, this is a city to browse and wander.

Department Store: Hema is at Nieuwstraat 13 (Mon–Sat 9:30–18:30, closed Sun, tel. 02-227-5210).

Laundry: There's a coin-op launderette at Rue du Midi 65 (daily 7:00–21:00, change machine).

Travel Agency and Discount Flights: The **Connections Agency** has a line on air and rail connections, including the Eurostar to London and the Thalys to Paris and Amsterdam (€10/person booking fee, Mon–Fri 9:30–18:30, opens Wed at 10:30, Sat 10:00–17:00, closed Sun, free coffee and WC, Rue du Midi 19–21, tel. 02-550-0130, www.connections.be).

Getting Around Brussels

Most of central Brussels' sights are walkable. But public transport is handy for connecting the train stations, climbing to the Upper Town (bus #95 from the Bourse), or visiting sights outside the central core. To reach these outlying sights, such as the European Parliament, take the Métro or jump on a hop-on, hop-off tour bus from Central Station (described under "Tours," next page; check tour bus route map to make sure it covers the sights you want to see). On summer weekends, a charming old-time trolley goes out to the Royal Museum of Central Africa.

By Métro, Bus, Tram, and Train: A single €1.50 ticket is good for one hour on all public transportation—Métro, buses, trams, and even trains shuttling between Brussels' three train stations (notice the time when you first stamp it, stamp it again if you transfer lines, buy single tickets on buses or at Métro stations). Deals are available at the TI at Rue de Marché-aux-Herbes 63 and at Métro stations: an all-day pass for €4.20 (cheaper than three single tickets; on Sat–Sun and holidays, this pass covers two people); or a 10-ride card for €11. The free *Métro Tram Bus Plan* is excellent; pick it up at either TI or any Métro station. In 2009, the Mobib swipe-card system will be introduced (similar to London's Oyster card), allowing you to use a "refillable" plastic card to pay for public transit (transit info: tel. 02-515-2000, www.mivb.be).

Brussels' Métro has three lines that run mostly east–west: 1A (Roi Baudouin-Debroux), 1B (Erasmus-Stokkel), and the circular 2 (Simonis-Clemenceau). A series of tram lines run north–south through the city center, connecting the Métro lines and the Nord, Central, and Midi train stations. Whether you're on a Métro train, bus, or tram, validate your ticket when you enter, feeding it into the breadbox-size orange machines.

Near the Grand Place are two transportation hubs: Central Station and the Bourse. Those staying in hotels northwest of the Grand Place have good access to the Métro system at the De Brouckère and Ste. Catherine stops.

By Taxi: Drivers in big-city Brussels are happy to take you for a ride; find out the approximate cost to your destination before you head out. Cabbies charge a €2.40 drop fee, as well as €1.35 per additional kilometer. After 22:00, you'll be hit with a €2 surcharge. You'll pay about €10 to ride from the center to the European Parliament. Convenient taxi stands are at the Bourse (near Grand Place) and at Place du Grand Sablon (in the Upper Town). To call a cab, try Taxi Bleu (tel. 02-268-0000).

TOURS

Hop-On, Hop-Off Bus Tours—Two different companies offer nearly identical "discovery" city tours. The 90-minute loop and recorded narration give you a once-over-lightly of the city from the top deck (open on sunny days) of a double-decker bus. While you can hop on and off for 24 hours with one ticket, schedules are sparse (about 2/hr, times listed on each flier; both companies run roughly April–Oct daily 10:00–16:00, Sat until 17:00; Nov–March daily 10:00–15:00, Sat until 16:00). Except for the trip out to the European Parliament and Cinquantenaire Park (which hosts the military and auto museums), I'd just stay on to enjoy the views and the minimal commentary. The fiercely competitive companies often both have hustlers at the Central Station trying to get you on board (offering "student" discounts to customers of all ages). The handiest starting points are the Central Station and the Bourse. The companies are **City Tours** (€18, tel. 02-513-7744, www.brussels-city-tours.com) and **Golden Tours** (€18, mobile 0486-053-981, www.goldentours.be).

Bus Tours—City Tours also offers a typical three-hour, guided (in up to five languages) bus tour, providing an easy way to get the grand perspective on Brussels. You start with a walk around the Grand Place, then jump on a tour bus (€27, year-round daily at 10:00 and 14:00, April–Oct extra tours Sat–Sun at 11:00; depart from their office a block off Grand Place at Rue du Marche aux Herbes 82; you can buy tickets there, at TI, or in your hotel; tel. 02-513-7744, www.brussels-city-tours.com). You'll get off the bus briefly at the Atomium for a quick photo stop.

Private Guide—Claude Janssens is good (€106/half-day, €200/day, mobile 0485-025-423, www.dobeltour.be, claude.janssens@pandora.be).

SIGHTS

On and near Grand Place

Brussels' Grand Place area sights, listed briefly below, are described in more detail in the ○ Grand Place Walk.

▲▲▲**Grand Place**—Brussels' main square, aptly called Grand Place (grahn plahs, "Grote Markt" in Flemish), is the heart of the old town and Brussels' greatest sight. Any time of day, it's worth swinging by to see what's going on. Concerts, flower markets, sound-and-light shows, endless people-watching—it entertains (as do the streets around it). The museums on the square are well-advertised, but dull.

Town Hall (Hôtel de Ville), with the tallest spire, is the square's centerpiece, but its interior is no big deal. Admission is only possible with a 40-minute English tour, which also covers city history and the building's tapestries and architecture (€3, Tue–Wed at 15:15, Sun at 10:45 and 12:15, no Sun tours Oct–March). Only 25 people are allowed per tour; assure a spot by buying tickets from the guide exactly 40 minutes before the tour starts (in the court-yard behind the spire).

The **City Museum** (Musée de la Ville de Bruxelles) is oppo-site Town Hall in an 1875 Neo-Gothic building called the *Maison du Roi*, or "King's House" (but no king ever lived here). The top floor displays a chronological history of the city and an enjoyable room full of costumes dampened by the *Manneken-Pis* statue. An engrossing video of tourist reactions to the statue plays constantly. The middle floor features maps and models of 13th- and 17th-century Brussels, and the bottom floor has tapestries and paintings (€3, Tue–Sun 10:00–17:00, closed Mon, Grand Place, tel. 02-279-4350). For local history, the best choice is not this museum—but the BELvue Museum.

BRUSSELS SIGHTS

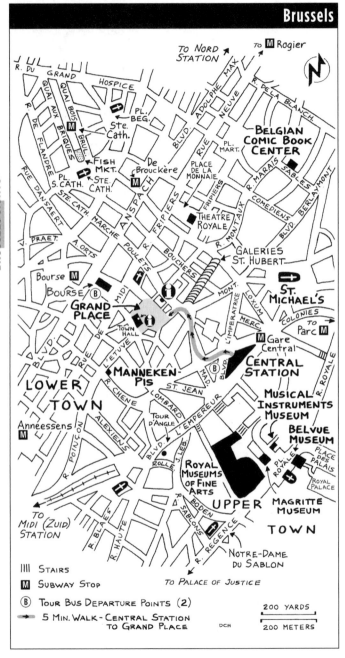

Brussels

TO NORD STATION

TO Ⓜ Rogier

R. DU GRAND HOSPICE

QUAI AUX BRIQUES

QUAI BOIS

BRÛL.

R. DE FLANDRE

RUE DANSAERT

Ⓜ

PL. BEG.

Ste. Cath.

FISH MKT.

PL. S. CATH.

Ste. CATH. Ⓜ

De Brouckère

ADOLPHE MAX

NEUVE

PL. MART.

PLACE DE LA MONNAIE

FRIPIERS

R. DE LA BLANCH.

BELGIAN COMIC BOOK CENTER

R. MARAIS

SABLES

BERLAYMONT

COMEDIENS

BLVD.

THEATRE ROYALE

MARCHE A ORTS

ANSPACH

MARCHE POULETS

BOUCHERS

R. MONTAGN.

GALERIES ST. HUBERT

PRAET.

Bourse Ⓜ

BOURSE Ⓑ

MIDI

ⓘ

GRAND PLACE

TOWN HALL

ⓘ

MONT.

L'IMPERATRICE

MERC.

ST. MICHAEL'S

COLONIES

TO Ⓜ Parc Ⓜ

Ⓜ Gare Central

CENTRAL STATION

R. ROYALE

LOWER TOWN

L'ETUVE

R. CHENE

MANNEKEN-PIS

ST. JEAN

LOMBARD

TOUR D'ANGLE

MAD

BLVD.

Ⓑ

MUSICAL INSTRUMENTS MUSEUM

BELVUE MUSEUM

Anneessens Ⓜ

ALEXIENS

L'EMPEREUR

J. LEB

ROLLE

BLVD.

ROYAL MUSEUMS OF FINE ARTS

PL. ROYALE

ROYAL PALACE

PLACE DES PALAIS

R. BLAES

R. HAUTE

R. SABLONS

BODEN

UPPER

MAGRITTE MUSEUM

TO MIDI (ZUID) STATION

R. REGENCE

TOWN

NOTRE-DAME DU SABLON

TO PALACE OF JUSTICE

|||| STAIRS

Ⓜ SUBWAY STOP

Ⓑ TOUR BUS DEPARTURE POINTS (2)

➡ 5 MIN. WALK - CENTRAL STATION TO GRAND PLACE

DCH

200 YARDS

200 METERS

N

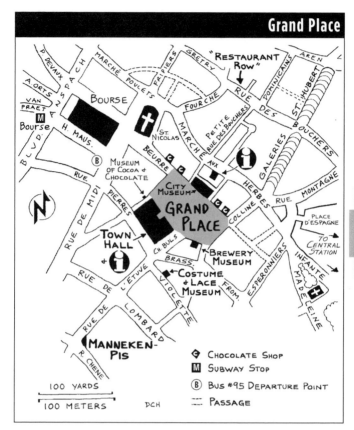

Grand Place

CHOCOLATE SHOP
SUBWAY STOP
BUS #95 DEPARTURE POINT
PASSAGE

The **Brewery Museum** has one room of old brewing para-phernalia and one room of new, plus a beer video in English. It's pretty lame...but a good excuse for a beer (€5 includes an unnamed local beer, daily 10:00–17:00, except Dec–March Sat–Sun opens at 12:00; Grand Place 10, tel. 02-511-4987).

The **Museum of Cocoa and Chocolate,** to the right of Town Hall, is a delightful concept. But it's overpriced at €5 for a meager set of displays, a second-rate video, a look at a "chocolate master" at work, and a choco-sample (daily 10:00–16:30, until 17:00 July–Aug, Rue de la Tête d'Or 9, www.mucc.be).

▲**Chocolate Shops on Grand Place**—For many, the best thing about Grand Place is the chocolate sold at the four venerable chocolate shops: Godiva, Neuhaus, Galler, and Leonidas (shops generally open Mon–Sat 9:00–22:00, Sun 10:00–22:00). Each has inviting displays and sells mixes of 100 grams (your choice of 6–8 pieces) or individual pieces for about €1.60. It takes a lot of

Brussels at a Glance

▲▲▲**Grand Place** Main square and spirited heart of the old town, surrounded by mediocre museums and delectable chocolate shops. **Hours:** Always open. See page 79.

▲▲▲**Royal Museums of Fine Arts of Belgium** Three museums in one, displaying ancient art (14th-18th centuries), modern art (19th-20th centuries), and works by Surrealist painter René Magritte. **Hours:** Ancient Art and Modern Art museums—Tue–Sun 10:00–17:00, closed Mon; Magritte Museum—Tue–Sun 9:30–17:00, Wed until 20:00, closed Mon. See page 84.

▲▲**BELvue Museum** Interesting Belgian history museum with a focus on the popular royal family. **Hours:** June–Sept Tue–Sun 10:00–18:00, Oct–May Tue–Sun 10:00–17:00, closed Mon year-round. See page 85.

▲▲**Royal Army and Military History Museum** Vast collection of weaponry and uniforms. **Hours:** Tue–Sun 9:00–16:45, closed Mon. See page 89.

▲**Chocolate on Grand Place** Choco-crawl through Godiva, Neuhaus, Galler, and Leonidas. **Hours:** Generally daily 9:00–22:00. See page 81.

▲**Musical Instruments Museum** More than 1,500 instruments, complete with audio. **Hours:** Tue–Fri 9:30–17:00, Sat–Sun 10:00–17:00, closed Mon. See page 85.

▲**St. Michael's Cathedral** White-stone Gothic church where Belgian royals are married and buried. **Hours:** Mon–Fri 7:00–18:00, Sat–Sun 8:30–18:00, until 19:00 in summer. See page 86.

▲**Belgian Comic Strip Center** Hometown heroes the Smurfs, Tintin, and Lucky Luke, plus many more. **Hours:** Tue–Sun 10:00–18:00, closed Mon. See page 86.

▲**European Parliament** Soaring home of Europe's governing body. **Hours:** Audioguide tours Mon–Thu at 10:00 and 15:00, also at 16:30 July-Aug; Fri at 10:00 only. See page 87.

Park of the Cinquantenaire Belgium's sprawling tribute to inde-pendence, near the European Parliament. **Hours:** Always open. See page 88.

▲**Autoworld** Hundreds of historic vehicles, including Mr. Benz's 1886 motorized tricycle. **Hours:** Daily April–Sept 10:00–18:00, Oct–March 10:00–17:00. See page 89.

▲**Royal Museum of Art and History** Filled with fine art, it's appropriately nicknamed "the local Louvre." **Hours:** Tue–Fri 9:30–17:00, Sat–Sun 10:00–17:00, closed Mon. See page 88.

▲**Royal Museum of Central Africa** Excellent but far-flung exhibit about the former Belgian Congo, featuring ethnology, artifacts, and wildlife. **Hours:** Tue–Fri 10:00–17:00, Sat–Sun 10:00–18:00, closed Mon. See page 90.

City Museum Costumes worn by the *Manneken-Pis* statue and models of Brussels' history. **Hours:** Tue–Sun 10:00–17:00, closed Mon. See page 79.

Costume and Lace Museum World-famous Brussels lace, as well as outfits, embroideries, and accessories from the 17th–20th cen-turies. **Hours:** Mon–Tue and Thu–Fri 10:00–12:30 & 13:30–17:00, Sat–Sun 14:00–17:00, closed Wed. See page 84.

Royal Belgian Institute of Natural Sciences Europe's largest dinosaur gallery. **Hours:** Tue–Fri 9:30–16:45, Sat–Sun 10:00–18:00, closed Mon. See page 90.

Atomium Fun space-age videos and displays, and an elevator ride to the panorama deck. **Hours:** Daily 10:00–19:00, later in summer. See page 90.

Mini-Europe Models of 350 famous European landmarks. **Hours:** Easter–Sept daily 9:30–18:00, July–Aug until 20:00; Oct–Dec 10:00–18:00; closed Jan-Easter. See page 90.

sampling to judge. See the "choco-crawl" described in the Grand Place Walk.

Manneken-Pis—Brussels is a great city with a cheesy mascot (apparently symbolizing the city's irreverence and love of the good life)—a statue of a little boy urinating. Read up on his story at any postcard stand. It's three short blocks off Grand Place, but, for exact directions, take my Grand Place Walk, look for small, white *Manneken-Pis* signs, or just ask a local, *"Où est le Manneken-Pis?"* The little squirt may be wearing some clever outfit, as costumes are sent to Brussels from around the world. Cases full of these are on display in the City Museum.

Costume and Lace Museum—This is worthwhile only to those who have devoted their lives to the making of lace (€3, Mon–Tue and Thu–Fri 10:00–12:30 & 13:30–17:00, Sat–Sun 14:00–17:00, closed Wed, Rue de la Violette 12, a block off Grand Place, tel. 02-213-4450).

Upper Town

Brussels' grandiose Upper Town, with its huge palace, is described in the ✪ Upper Town Walk. Along that walk, you'll pass the following sights.

▲▲▲Royal Museums of Fine Arts of Belgium (Musées Royaux des Beaux-Arts de Belgique)—This sprawling complex is worth visiting for the three museums that hold its permanent collection.

The **Museum of Ancient Art** and the **Museum of Modern Art** are covered by the same €5 ticket (enter through the main foyer for both). The Museum of Ancient Art—featuring Flemish and Belgian art of the 14th–18th centuries—is packed with a dazzling collection of masterpieces by Van der Weyden, Brueghel, Bosch, and Rubens. The Museum of Modern Art gives an easy-to-enjoy walk through the art of the 19th and 20th centuries, from Neoclassical to Surrealism. Highlights here include works by Seurat, Gauguin, and David (Tue–Sun 10:00–17:00, closed Mon, last entry at 16:30, audioguide-€2.50, tour booklet-€2.50, pricey cafeteria with salad bar, Rue de la Régence 3, recorded info tel. 02-508-3211, www.fine-arts-museum.be).

The new **Magritte Museum,** honoring the Surrealist painter René Magritte, opens in the same museum complex in 2009 and contains over 150 works housed on three floors of a Neoclassical building (separate €8 ticket, Tue–Sun 9:30–17:00, Wed until 20:00, closed Mon). The Magritte Museum is the best art news in Brussels. Magritte's works are best described in his own words: *"My paintings are visible images which conceal nothing; they evoke mystery and, indeed, when one sees one of my pictures, one asks oneself this simple question, 'What does that mean'? It does not mean anything,* *because mystery means nothing either, it is unknowable."*

❂ See Royal Museums of Fine Arts of Belgium Tour.

▲**Musical Instruments Museum (Musée des Instruments de Musique)**—One of Europe's best music museums (nicknamed "MIM") is housed in one of Brussels' most impressive Art Nouveau buildings, the newly renovated Old English department store. Inside, you'll be given a pair of headphones and set free to

wander several levels: folk instruments from around the world on the ground floor, a history of Western musical instruments on the first, and an entire floor devoted to strings and pianos on the second. Part of the **Royal Museum of Art and History** (described later in this chapter), this museum has more than 1,500 instruments—from Egyptian harps, to medieval lutes, to groundbreaking harpsichords, to the Brussels-built saxophone.

As you approach an instrument, you hear it playing on your headphones (which actually work...most of the time). The museum is skimpy on English information—except for a laminated sheet in each section that simply identifies instruments—but the music you'll hear is an international language (€5, Tue–Fri 9:30–17:00, Sat–Sun 10:00–17:00, closed Mon, last entry 45 min before closing, Rue Montagne de la Cour 2, just downhill and toward Grand Place from the Royal Museums of Fine Arts, tel. 02-545-0130, www.mim.fgov.be). The sixth floor has a restaurant, a terrace, and a great view of Brussels (€10–15 *plats du jour*, same hours as museum, pick up free access pass at museum entrance).

▲▲**BELvue Museum**—This brilliant museum, which fills two palatial floors, offers far and away the best look in town at Belgian history. The exhibit, with lots of real historical artifacts, illustrates the short sweep of this nation's story, from its 1830 inception to

today: kings, its bloody reign in the Congo, Art Nouveau, and world wars. The rooms proceed in chronological order, and outside in the hallway, displays on the monarchy provide a chance to get to know the generally much-loved royal family with intimate family photos. To make the most of your visit, follow along with the wonderful and extensive flier translating all of the descriptions (€3, €5 combo-ticket includes Coudenberg

Palace; June–Sept Tue–Sun 10:00–18:00, Oct–May Tue–Sun 10:00–17:00, closed Mon year-round, to the right of the palace at place des Palais 7, tel. 07-022-0492, www.belvue.be). Lunch is served in the lobby of this former princess' palace (€10–15 plates, same hours as museum).

Coudenberg Palace—The BELvue Museum stands atop the barren archaeological remains of a 12th-century Brussels palace. While well-lit and well-described, the ruins still aren't much to see. The best thing is the free orientation video you see before descending (€4, €5 combo-ticket includes BELvue Museum, same hours as BELvue).

North of Central Station

▲**St. Michael's Cathedral**—Belgium is largely Catholic, and St. Michael's Cathedral has been the center of Belgium's religious life for nearly 1,000 years. While the Netherlands went in

a Protestant direction in the 1500s, Belgium remains 80 percent Catholic (although only about 20 percent go to Mass). One of Europe's classic Gothic churches, built between roughly 1200 and 1500, Brussels' cathedral is made from white stone and topped by twin towers (Mon–Fri 7:00–18:00, Sat–Sun 8:30–18:00, until 19:00 in summer).

The church is where royal weddings and funerals take place. Photographs (to the right of the entrance) show the funeral of the popular King Baudouin, who died in 1993. He was succeeded by his younger brother, Albert II (whose face is on Belgium's euro coins). Albert will be succeeded by his son, Prince Philippe. Traditionally, the ruler was always a man, but in 1992 the constitution was changed, making it clear that the oldest child—boy or girl—would take the throne. In 1999, Prince Philippe and his bride, Mathilde—after a civil ceremony at the Town Hall—paraded up here for a two-hour Catholic ceremony with all the trimmings. They had a baby girl in 2001, and she is in line to become Belgium's Queen Elisabeth.

Before leaving, enjoy the great view from the outside porch of the Town Hall spire with its gold statue of St. Michael.

▲**Belgian Comic Strip Center (Centre Belge de la Bande Dessinée)**—Belgium has produced some of the world's most popular comic characters, including the Smurfs, Tintin, and Lucky Luke. You'll find these, and many less famous local comics, at the Comic Strip Center.

Just pop into the lobby to see the museum's groundbreaking

Art Nouveau building (a former department store designed in 1903 by Belgian architect Victor Horta), browse through comics

in the bookshop, and snap a photo with a three-foot-tall Smurf...and that's enough for many people. Kids especially might find the museum, like, totally boring. But those who appreciate art in general will enjoy this sometimes humorous, sometimes probing, often beautiful medium. The displays are in French and Flemish, but they loan out a helpful, if hard-to-follow, English guidebook.

You'll see how comics are made, watch early animated films (such as *Gertie the Dinosaur,* c. 1909), and see a sprawling exhibit on Tintin (the intrepid boy reporter with the button eyes and wavy shock of hair, launched in 1929 by Hergé and much loved by older Europeans). The top floor is dedicated to "serious" comics, where more adult themes and high-quality drawing aspire to turn kids' stuff into that "Ninth Art." These works can be grimly realistic, openly erotic or graphic, or darker in tone, featuring flawed anti-heroes (€7.50, Tue–Sun 10:00–18:00, closed Mon, 10-minute walk from Grand Place to Rue des Sables 20, tel. 02-219-1980, www.comicscenter.net).

▲**European Parliament**—Europe's governing body welcomes visitors with an information center and audioguide tours. This towering complex of glass skyscrapers is a cacophony of black-suited

politicians speaking 20 different Euro-languages. It's exciting just to be here—a mouse in the corner of a place that aspires to chart the future of Europe "with respect for all political thinking...consolidating democracy in the spirit of peace and solidarity." The 785 parliament members, representing 28 countries and 457 million citizens, shape Europe with a €120 billion budget (from import duties, sales taxes, and a cut of each member country's GDP).

The **Info Point** is a welcoming place with 28 flags, entertaining racks of freebies, and videos promoting the concept and beauties of the European Union (including bins of tiny *My Fundamental Rights in the EU* booklets). Ask for the *Troubled Waters* comic book, which explains how the parliament works (free, Mon–Fri 9:00–17:15, closed Sat–Sun, www.europarl.europa.eu).

An adjacent, bigger-and-even-better center is planned for 2009.

Audioguide tours, the only way to get inside the European Parliament, leave from the Info Point office (free, Mon–Thu at 10:00 and 15:00, also at 16:30 July–Aug; Fri only at 10:00; confirm tour time by calling 02-284-2111, arrive 30 min early, no visitors under 14 years old).

At the appointed time, enter the main hall through the double doors and meet your escort, who equips you with an audioguide and takes you to a balcony overlooking the huge "hemi-cycle" where the members of the European Parliament sit. Here you'll listen to a political-science lesson about the all-Europe system of governance. You'll learn how early visionary utopians (like Churchill, who in 1946 called for a "United States of Europe" to avoid future wars) led the way as Europe gradually evolved into the European Union (1992).

Getting There: The European Parliament is next to Place du Luxembourg. From the Bourse in downtown Brussels, take bus #95; from the museums at the Park of the Cinquantenaire or the Royal Palace, take bus #27. From Place du Luxembourg, go behind the old train station and look for the *Info Point* sign.

Park of the Cinquantenaire (Parc du Cinquantenaire)—The 19th-century Belgian king Leopold wanted Brussels to rival Paris. In 1880, he celebrated the 50th anniversary (cinquantenaire) of Belgian independence by building a huge monumental arch flanked by massive exhibition halls, which today house the Royal Museum of Art and History, Autoworld, and the military museum (see next listings). The Métro stop is 200 yards from the museums (follow signs to museum and walk to the statue crowning the big arch).

Connecting to Other Sights: If seeing both the Park of the Cinquantenaire and the European Parliament, take advantage of the wonderful public transportation connections that make this easy. The Métro zips you from the center out to the park in minutes (Métro stop: Merode). From the park (Métro stop: Gaulois), bus #27 runs four times an hour to the Luxembourg stop (for the European Parliament) and on to the Royal stop (for the Royal Palace and great nearby museums). It's cheap and easy, plus you'll feel quite clever doing it.

▲**Royal Museum of Art and History**—This is the "Belgian Louvre," with an impressive collection split between two wings: European items in one wing, and antiquities and items from beyond Europe in the other. In the Europe wing, the basement takes you from pre-history, to Roman artifacts, to medieval Belgian. The ground floor is a chronological walk from Gothic to Renaissance to Baroque. Wandering the almost empty halls, you'll see fine tapestries, exquisite altarpieces, an impressive Islamic collection, Art Nouveau, and a "museum of the heart" donated by a local heart doctor. Unfortunately, the museum entrance is hidden behind Autoworld (€4, free and necessary audioguide, Tue–Fri 9:30–17:00, Sat–Sun 10:00–17:00, closed Mon; Jubelpark 10, Parc du Cinquantenaire, bus #27 goes to the Gaulois Métro stop a block away; tel. 02-741-7211).

▲**Autoworld**—Starting with Mr. Benz's motorized tricycle of 1886, you'll stroll through a giant hall filled with 400 historic cars.

Car buffs can ogle circa-1905 models from Peugeot, Renault, Oldsmobile, Cadillac, and Rolls-Royce. It's well-described in English (€6, daily April–Sept 10:00–18:00, Oct–March 10:00–17:00, in Palais Mondial, Parc du Cinquantenaire 11, Métro: Merode, tel. 02-736-4165, www.auto world.be).

▲▲**Royal Army and Military History Museum (Musée Royal de l'Armée et d'Histoire Militaire)**—Wander through an enormous collection of 19th-century weaponry and uniforms, and a giant hall dedicated to warplanes of the 20th century. There's a good display about the Belgian struggle for independence in the early 1800s and the best collection of WWI weaponry anywhere. Don't miss the primitive WWI tanks—able to break through the stalemated "Western Front," but so clumsy that they couldn't do anything once in enemy ter-

ritory. This place is filled with real, tangible history...but precious little English. Use the map and pay €3 for the essential audioguide to get the most out of your visit (free, Tue–Sun 9:00–16:45, closed Mon, Parc du Cinquantenaire 3, tel. 02-737-7811, www.klm-mra .be). While sections of the museum close from 12:00 to 13:00, most of it stays open.

Other Museums and Sights Away from the Center

Royal Belgian Institute of Natural Sciences (Institut Royal des Sciences Naturelles de Belgique)—Dinosaur enthusiasts come to this museum for the world's largest collection of iguanodon skeletons (€7, Tue–Fri 9:30–16:45, Sat–Sun 10:00–18:00, closed Mon, last entry 30 min before closing, Rue Vautier 29, bus #34 from the Bourse, tel. 02-627-4238, www.naturalsciences.be).

▲**Royal Museum of Central Africa (Musée Royal de l'Afrique Centrale)**—Remember the Belgian Congo? Just east of the city center, this fine museum covers the Congo and much more of Africa, including ethnography, sculpture, jewelry, colonial history, flora, and fauna. You'll learn about both the history of Belgian adventure in the Congo (when it was the king's private plantation) and the region's natural wonders. Unfortunately, there's barely a word of English (€4, Tue–Fri 10:00–17:00, Sat–Sun 10:00–18:00, closed Mon, Leuvensesteenweg 13, tel. 02-769-5211, www.africamuseum.be). The museum, housed in an immense palace, is surrounded by a vast and well-kept park. A trip out here puts you in a lush, wooded oasis a world away from the big, noisy city. To get here, take Métro #1B to Montgomery (direction: Stockel), and then catch tram #44 to its final stop, Tervuren. From there, walk 200 yards through the park to the palace.

Atomium—This giant, silvery iron molecule, with escalators connecting the various "atoms" and a view from the top sphere, was the über-optimistic symbol of the 1958 Universal Exhibition. Recently reopened after an extensive renovation, the Atomium now celebrates its kitschy past with fun space-age videos and displays. Your ticket includes an elevator ride to the panorama deck, as well as endless escalators and stairs. If you're scared of heights or tight spaces, tell your friends you'll wave to them... from the ground (€9, daily 10:00–19:00, later in summer, last entry one hour before closing,  on outskirts of town, Métro: Heysel and walk 5 min, tel. 02-475-4777, www.atomium.be).

Mini-Europe—This kid-pleasing sight, sharing a park with the Atomium, has 1:25-scale models of 350 famous European landmarks, such as Big Ben, the Eiffel Tower, and Venice. The new "Spirit of Europe" section is an interactive educational exhibit about the European Union (€13, Easter–Sept daily 9:30–18:00, July–Aug until 20:00, Oct–Dec 10:00–18:00, last entry one hour before closing, closed Jan–Easter, Métro: Heysel and walk 5 min, following signs to *Brupark*, tel. 02-474-1313, www.minieurope.com).

GRAND PLACE WALK

This walk takes in Brussels' delightful old center. After exploring the Grand Place itself, we'll loop a couple blocks north, see the Bourse, and then end south of the Grand Place at the *Manneken-Pis*.

ORIENTATION

Length of This Walk: Allow two hours.

Brewery Museum: €5, daily 10:00–17:00, except Dec–March opens on Sat–Sun at 12:00, Grand Place 10, tel. 02-511-4987.

City Museum: €3, Tue–Sun 10:00–17:00, closed Mon, Grand Place, tel. 02-279-4350.

Chocolate Shops: Generally open Mon–Sat 9:00–22:00, Sun 10:00–22:00, along the north side of the Grand Place.

Church of St. Nicolas: Rue de Tabora 6, tel. 02-513-8022.

THE WALK BEGINS

The Grand Place

This colorful cobblestone square is the heart—historically and geographically—of heart-shaped Brussels. As the town's market square for 1,000 years, this was where farmers and merchants sold their wares in open-air stalls, enticing travelers from the main east–west highway across Belgium, which ran a block north of the square. Today, shops and cafés sell chocolates, *gaufres* (waffles), beer, mussels, fries, lace, and flowers.

Brussels was born about 1,000 years ago around a long-gone castle put up by Germans to fight off the French (long before either of those countries actually existed). The villagers supplied the needs of the soldiers, and a city grew up on the banks of the Senne

The Grand Place: Center of Brussels

Face the Town Hall, with your back to the King's House. You're facing roughly southwest. The TI is one block behind you, and "restaurant row" is another block beyond that. To your right, a block away, catch a glimpse of the Bourse building (with buses, taxis, cafés). The Upper Town is to your left, rising up the hill beyond the Central Station. Over your left shoulder a few blocks away is St. Michael's Cathedral. And most important? The *Manneken-Pis* is three blocks ahead, down the street that runs along the left side of the Town Hall.

(not Seine) River, which today is completely bricked over. The river crossed the main road from Köln to Bruges.

Pan the square to get oriented. The **Town Hall** (Hôtel de

Ville) dominates the square with its 300-foot-tall tower, topped by a golden statue of St. Michael slaying a devil (skippable interior). This was where the city council met to rule this free trading town. Brussels proudly maintained its self-governing independence while dukes, kings, and clergymen ruled much of Europe. These days, the Town Hall hosts weddings—Crown Prince Philippe got married here in 1999. (The Belgian government demands

that all marriages first be performed in simple civil ceremonies.)

Opposite the Town Hall is the impressive, gray **King's House** (Maison du Roi), used by the Habsburg kings not as a house, but as an administrative center. Rebuilt in the 1890s, it's a stately and prickly Neo-Gothic building. Inside is the mildly interesting City Museum.

The fancy smaller buildings giving the square its uniquely grand medieval character are former **guild halls** (now mostly shops and restaurants), their impressive gabled roofs topped with statues. Once the home offices for the town's different professions (bakers, brewers, tanners, and *Manneken-Pis*-corkscrewmakers), they all date from shortly after 1695—the year French king

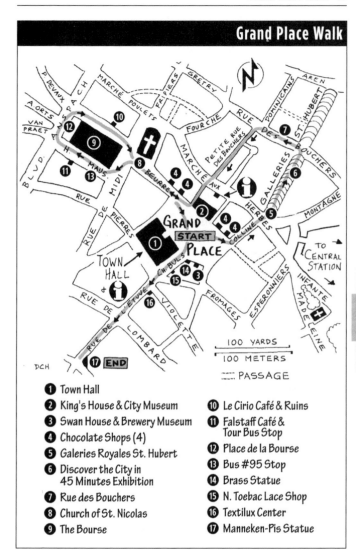

Grand Place Walk

❶ Town Hall
❷ King's House & City Museum
❸ Swan House & Brewery Museum
❹ Chocolate Shops (4)
❺ Galeries Royales St. Hubert
❻ Discover the City in 45 Minutes Exhibition
❼ Rue des Bouchers
❽ Church of St. Nicolas
❾ The Bourse
❿ Le Cirio Café & Ruins
⓫ Falstaff Café & Tour Bus Stop
⓬ Place de la Bourse
⓭ Bus #95 Stop
⓮ Brass Statue
⓯ N. Toebac Lace Shop
⓰ Textilux Center
⓱ Manneken-Pis Statue

Louis XIV's troops surrounded the city, sighted their cannons on the Town Hall spire, and managed to level everything around it (4,000 wooden buildings) without ever hitting the spire itself. As a matter of pride, these Brussels businessmen rebuilt their offices better than ever, completing everything within seven years. They're in stone, taller, and with ornamented gables and classical statues.

The **Swan House** (#9, just to the left of the Town Hall) once housed a bar where Karl Marx and Friedrich Engels met in February of 1848 to write their *Communist Manifesto.* Later that year, when the treatise sparked socialist revolution around Europe, Brussels exiled them. Today, the once-proletarian bar is one of the city's most expensive restaurants. Next door (#10) was and still is the brewers' guild, now housing the **Brewery Museum**.

The **statues** on the rooftops each come with their own uninteresting legend, but the Bruxelloise have an earthier explanation:

"What's that smell?" say the statues on the roof of the Swan House. "Someone farted." "Yeah," says the golden man riding a horse atop the Brewery Museum next door, "it was that guy over there," and he points north across the square to another statue. "It wasn't me," says that statue, "it was him—way over there." Follow his gaze to the southwest corner of the square, where a statue of St. Nicolas...hangs his head in shame.

• *In the King's House (across from the Town Hall) is the only museum of any importance on the square...*

City Museum

The museum's top floor has a roomful of goofy costumes the *Manneken* statue has pissed through, the middle floor features maps and models of old Brussels, and the bottom floor has a few old paintings, fine carved altarpieces, and tapestries. On the ground floor, you'll see the original statues that once adorned the Town Hall. The local limestone is no match for the corrosive acidic air, so they were brought inside for protection. Most visitors aim straight for the *Manneken-Pis* outfits. Once up there,

sit down and enjoy the video showing visitors' reactions to the ridiculous little statue.

But be sure to find the model of the city in the 13th century, on the second floor. (To follow the directions in this description, uphill is east.) The largest structure is St. Michael's Cathedral (northeast). The Upper Town hasn't a hint of its monumental future. The Grand Place's embryonic beginning is roughly in the center of town, amid a cluster of houses.

The city was a port town—see the crane unloading barges—since it was at this point that the shallow Senne became navigable. Grain from the area was processed in the watermills, then shipped downstream to the North Sea.

By the 1200s, Brussels—though tiny by today's standards—was an important commercial center, and St. Michael's was the region's religious hub. Still, most of the area inside the 2.5-mile-long city wall was farmland, dotted with a few churches, towers, markets, and convents (such as the Carmelite convent hugging the south wall).

The model in the far end of the room shows the city a couple centuries later—much bigger, but still within the same wall. By this time, the Upper and Lower Towns are clearly defined. In the Upper Town, the huge palace of the dukes of Burgundy marks the site of today's Royal Palace.

Taste Treats on the Grand Place

Cafés: Mussels in Brussels, Belgian-style french fries, yeasty local beers, waffles...if all you do is plop down at a café on the square, try some of these specialties, and watch the world go by—hey, that's a great afternoon in Brussels.

The outdoor cafés are casual and come with fair prices (a good Belgian beer costs €3.50—with no cover or service charge). Have a seat, and a waiter will serve you. The half-dozen or so cafés are all roughly equal in price and quality for simple drinks and foods—check the posted menus.

Choco-Crawl: The best chocolate shops all lie along the north (uphill) side of the square, starting with Godiva at the high end (that is, higher in both altitude and price). The cost goes down slightly as you descend to the other shops. Each shop has a mouth-watering display case of 20 or so chocolates and sells mixes of 100 grams—your choice of 6–8 pieces—for about €5, or individual pieces for about €1.60. Pralines are filled chocolates—uniquely Belgian (and totally different from the French praline). The shops are generally open daily from 9:00 to 22:00 (opening at 10:00 Sun).

Godiva, with the top reputation internationally, is synonymous with fine Belgian chocolate. Now owned by an American, Godiva still has its management and the original factory (built in 1926) in Belgium. This store, at Grand Place 22, was Godiva's first (est. 1937). The almond and honey goes way beyond almond roca.

Neuhaus, a few doors down at #27, has been encouraging local chocoholics since 1857. Look through the glass floor at the old-time choco-kitchen in the basement, and check out the historic photos on the walls. The enticing varieties are described in English, and Neuhaus publishes a fine little pamphlet (free, on the counter) explaining the products. The "caprice" (toffee with vanilla crème) tastes like Easter. Neuhaus claims to be the inventor of the filled chocolate.

GRAND PLACE WALK

History of Chocolate

In 1519, Montezuma served Cortés a cup of hot cocoa *(xocoatl)* made from cocoa beans, which were native to the New World. It ignited a food fad in Europe—by 1700, elegant "chocolate houses" in Europe's capitals served hot chocolate (with milk and sugar added) to wealthy aristocrats. By the 1850s, the process of making chocolate candies for eating was developed, and Brussels, with a long tradition of quality handmade luxuries, was at the forefront.

Cocoa beans are husked, fermented, and roasted, then ground into chocolate paste. (Chocolate straight from the bean is very bitter.) The vegetable fat is pressed out to make cocoa butter. Cocoa butter and chocolate paste are mixed together and sweetened with sugar to make chocolates. In 1876, a Swiss man named Henry Nestlé added concentrated milk, creating milk chocolate—a lighter, sweeter variation, with less pure chocolate.

Galler, just off the square at Rue au Beurre 44, is homier and less famous because it doesn't export. Still family-run (and the royal favorite), it proudly serves less sugary chocolate—dark. The new top-end choice, 85 percent pure chocolate, is called simply "Black 85"—and worth a sample if you like chocolate without the sweetness. Galler's products are well-described in English.

At **Leonidas,** four doors down at Rue au Beurre 34, most locals sacrifice 10 percent in quality to double their take by getting their fix here (machine-made, only €1.60/100 grams). White chocolate is the specialty.

• *Exit the Grand Place next to Godiva (from the northeast, or uphill, corner of the square), and go north one block on Rue de la Colline (passing a popular Tintin shop at #13 and a Europe shop across the street) to Rue du Marché-aux-Herbes, which was once the main east–west highway through Belgium. Looking to the right, notice that it's all uphill from here to the Upper Town, another four blocks (and 200-foot elevation gain) beyond. Straight ahead, you enter the arcaded shopping mall called...*

Galeries Royales St. Hubert

Europe's oldest still-operating shopping mall, built in 1847, served as the glass-covered model that inspired many other malls. It celebrated the town's new modern attitude (having recently gained its independence from the Netherlands). Built in an age of expan-

sion and industrialization, the mall demonstrated efficient modern living, with elegant apartments upstairs above fine shops, theaters, and cafés. Originally, you had to pay to get in to see its fancy shops—that elite sensibility survives today.

Looking down the arcade, you'll notice that it bends halfway down, designed to lure shoppers further. Its iron-and-glass look is still popular today, but the decorative columns, cameos, and pastel colors evoke a more elegant time. It's Neo-Renaissance, like a pastel Florentine palace.

There's no Gap (yet), no Foot Locker, no Karmelkorn. Instead, you'll find hat, cane, and, umbrella stores that sell...hats, canes, and umbrellas—that's it, all made on the premises. At **Philippe,** have shoes made especially for the curves of your feet by a family that's done it for generations. Since 1857, **Neuhaus** has sold chocolates from here at its flagship store, where many locals buy their pralines. Across from Neuhaus, the **Taverne du Passage** restaurant serves the same local specialties that singer Jacques Brel used to come here for: *croquettes de crevettes* (shrimp croquettes), *tête de veau* (calf's head), *anguilles au vert* (eels with herb sauce), and *fondue au fromage* (cheese fondue; €10–20 meals, daily 12:00–24:00).

The **Brussels Discover the City in 45 Minutes Exhibition** (see the sign midway down the gallery) is the strangest thing: You enter through the back of a chocolate shop and descend into a huge underground exhibit that cleverly and artistically gives you the sweep of the city with fine English descriptions (€6, daily 10:00–17:00, tel. 02-512-5745).

• *Midway down the mall, where the two sections bend, turn left and exit the mall onto...*

Rue des Bouchers

Yikes! During meal times, this street is absolutely crawling with tourists browsing through wall-to-wall, midlevel-quality restaurants. Brussels is known worldwide for its food, serving all kinds of cuisine, but specializing in seafood (particularly mussels). You'll have plenty to choose from along this table-clogged "restaurant row." To get an idea of prices, compare their posted *menùs*—the fixed-price, several-course meal offered by most restaurants.

Many diners here are day-trippers. Colin from London, Marie from Paris, Martje from Holland, and Dietrich from Bonn could

GRAND PLACE WALK

easily all "do lunch" together in Brussels—just three hours away.

The first intersection, with Petite Rue des Bouchers, is the heart of the restaurant quarter (and home to the recommended Chez Leon), which sprawls for several blocks around. The street names tell what sorts of shops used to stand here—butchers *(bouchers)*, herbs, chickens, and cheese.

• *At this intersection, turn left onto Petite Rue des Bouchers and walk straight back to the Grand Place. (You'll see the City Hall tower ahead.) At the Grand Place, turn right (west) on Rue du Beurre. Comparison-shop a little more at the Galler and Leonidas chocolate stores and pass by the "Is it raining?" fountain. A block along, at the intersection with Rue du Midi, is the...*

Church of St. Nicolas

Since the 12th century, there's been a church here. Inside, see rough stones in some of the arches from the early church. Outside, notice the barnacle-like shops, such as De Witte Jewelers, built right into the church. The church was rebuilt 300 years ago with money provided by the town's jewelers. As thanks, they were given these shops with apartments upstairs. Close to God, this was prime real estate. And jewelers are still here.

• *Just west of the church, the big Neoclassical building you run into is the back entrance of...*

The Bourse (Stock Exchange) and Art Nouveau Cafés

The stock exchange was built in the 1870s in a Neo-everything style. Several **historic cafés** huddle around the Bourse. To the right is the woody, atmospheric Le Cirio with its delightful circa-1900 interior, and to the left is the Falstaff Café. Some Brussels cafés, like the Falstaff, are still decorated in the early-20th-century style called Art Nouveau. Ironwork columns twist and bend like flower stems, and lots of Tiffany-style stained glass and mirrors make them light and spacious. Slender, elegant, willowy Gibson Girls decorate the wallpaper, while waiters in bowties glide by.

The **ruins** under glass on the right side of the Bourse are from a 13th-century convent.

• *Circle around to the front of the Bourse, toward the busy Boulevard Anspach. Note that the street in front of the Falstaff Café is a convenient place to catch a hop-on, hop-off bus tour.*

Place de la Bourse and Boulevard Anspach

Brussels is the political nerve center of Europe (only Washington, D.C., has more lobbyists), and the city sees several hundred demonstrations a year. When the local team wins a soccer match or some political group wants to make a statement, this is where people flock to wave flags and honk horns.

It's also where the old town meets the new. To the right along Boulevard Anspach are two shopping malls and several first-run movie theaters. Rue Neuve, which parallels Anspach, is a pedestrian-only shopping street.

Boulevard Anspach covers the still-flowing Senne River (which was open until 1850). Remember that Brussels was once a port, with North Sea boats coming as far as this point to unload their goods. But with frequent cholera epidemics killing thousands of its citizens, the city decided to cover up its stinky river.

• *For efficient sightseeing, consider catching bus #95 from alongside the Bourse (on Rue Henri Maus, just east of Falstaff Café) to the Place Royale, where you can follow my Upper Town Walk, also ending at the* Manneken-Pis. *But if you'd rather stay in the Lower Town, return to the Grand Place.*

From the Grand Place to the *Manneken-Pis*

• *Leave the square kitty-corner, heading south down the street running along the left side of the Town Hall, Rue Charles Buls (which soon*

changes its name to Stoofstraat). Just five yards off the square, under the arch, is a well-polished, well-loved brass statue.

You'll see tourists and locals rubbing a **brass statue** of a reclining man. This was Mayor Evrard 't Serclaes, who in 1356 bravely refused to surrender the keys of the city to invaders, and so was tortured and killed. Touch him, and his misfortune becomes your good luck. Judging by the reverence with which locals go through this ritual, there must be something to it.

The **N. Toebac Lace Shop** is a welcoming place with fine

lace, a knowledgeable staff, and an interesting three-minute video. Brussels is perhaps the best-known city for traditional lacemaking, and this shop still sells handmade pieces in the old style: lace clothing, doilies, tablecloths, and ornamental pieces (daily 9:30–19:30, Rue Charles Buls 10). The shop gives travelers with this book a 15 percent discount. If you spend more than €125, you get a further 13 percent tax rebate. For more

GRAND PLACE WALK

Lace

In the 1500s, rich men and women decided that lace collars, sleeves, headdresses, and veils were fashionable. For the next 200 years, the fashion raged (peaking in about 1700). All this lace had to be made by hand, and many women earned extra income from the demand. The French Revolution of 1789 suddenly made lace for men undemocratic and unmanly. Then, in about 1800, machines replaced human hands, and except for ornamental pieces, the fashion died out.

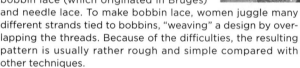

These days, handmade lace is usually also homemade—not produced in factories, but at home by dedicated, sharp-eyed hobbyists who love their work. Unlike knitting, it requires total concentration as they follow intricate patterns. Women create their own patterns or trace tried-and-true designs. A piece of lace takes days, not hours, to make—which is why a handmade tablecloth can easily sell for €250.

There are two basic kinds of lace: bobbin lace (which originated in Bruges) and needle lace. To make bobbin lace, women juggle many different strands tied to bobbins, "weaving" a design by overlapping the threads. Because of the difficulties, the resulting pattern is usually rather rough and simple compared with other techniques.

Needle lace is more like sewing—stitching pre-made bits onto a pattern. For example, the "Renaissance" design is made by sewing a pre-made ribbon onto a pattern in a fancy design. This would then be attached as a fringe to a piece of linen—to make a fancy tablecloth, for instance.

In the "Princess" design, pre-made pieces are stitched onto a cotton net, making anything from a small doily to a full wedding veil.

"Rose point"—no longer practiced—used authentic bits of handmade antique lace as an ornament in a frame or filling a pendant. Antique pieces can be very expensive.

on lace, the Costume and Lace Museum is a block away and just around the corner.

A block farther down the street, passing the always popular Waffle Factory (€4, freshly made, take-away, lots of fun toppings) step into the **Textilux Center** (Rue Lombard 41) for a good look at Belgian tapestries—both traditional wall-hangings and modern goods, such as tapestry purses and luggage in traditional designs.

• *Follow the crowds, noticing the excitement build, as in another block you reach the...*

Tapestries

In 1500, tapestry workshops in Brussels were famous, cranking out high-quality tapestries for the walls of Europe's palaces. They were functional (as insulation and propaganda for a church, king, or nobleman) and beautiful—an intricate design formed by colored thread. Even great painters (such as Rubens and Raphael) designed tapestries, which rivaled Renaissance canvases.

First, neutral-colored threads (made from imported English wool) are stretched vertically over a loom. The design of the tapestry is created with the horizontal weave, from the colored threads that (mostly) overlay the vertical threads. Tapestry-making is much more difficult than basic weaving because each horizontal thread is only as long as the detail it's meant to create, so a single horizontal row can be made up of many individual pieces of thread. The weavers follow a pattern designed by an artist, called a "cartoon."

Flanders and Paris (the Gobelins workshop) were the two centers of tapestry-making until the art died out, along with Europe's noble class.

Manneken-Pis

Even with low expectations, this bronze statue is smaller than

you'd think—the little squirt's under two feet tall, practically the size of a newborn. Still, the little peeing boy is an appropriately low-key symbol for the unpretentious Bruxelloise. The statue was made in 1619 to provide drinking water for the neighborhood. Sometimes, *Manneken-Pis* is dressed in one of the 700 different costumes that visiting VIPs have brought for him (including an Elvis Pissley outfit).

There are several different legends about *Manneken*—take your pick. He was a naughty boy who peed inside a witch's house, so she froze him. A rich man lost his son and declared, "Find my son, and we'll make a statue of him doing what he did when found." Or—the locals' favorite version—the little tyke loved his beer, which came in handy when a fire threatened the wooden city: He bravely put it out. Want

the truth? The city commissioned it to show the joie de vivre of living in Brussels—where happy people eat, drink...and drink... and then pee.

The scene is made interesting by the crowds that gather. Hang out for a while and watch the commotion this little guy makes as tour groups come and go. When I was there, a Russian man marveled at the statue, shook his head, and said, "He never stop!"

UPPER TOWN WALK

The Upper Town has always had a more aristocratic feel than the medieval, commercial streets of the Lower Town. With broad boulevards, big marble buildings, palaces, museums, and so many things called "royal," it also seems much newer and a bit more sterile. But in fact, the Upper Town has a history that stretches back to Brussels' beginnings.

Use this 10-stop walk to get acquainted with this less-touristed part of town, sample some world-class museums, see the palace, explore art galleries, and stand on a viewpoint to get the lay of the land.

The tour starts half a block from the one essential art sight in town, the Royal Museums of Fine Arts of Belgium, which include museums of ancient and modern art, and—new in 2009—the Magritte Museum. Consider a visit while you're here. The Musical Instruments Museum is also in the neighborhood (also closed Mon).

ORIENTATION

Length of This Walk: Allow 90 minutes.

Getting There: The walk begins at Place Royale in the Upper Town. You have several ways to get there:

    1. From the Grand Place, it's a 15-minute uphill walk (follow your map).

    2. From the Bourse, in front of the Falstaff Café, bus #95 leaves every few minutes for Place Royale (bus signs call it *Royale;* buy ticket from driver, validate it in machine).

    3. Catch a taxi (figure on €6 from the Bourse).

    4. Hop off here during a hop-on, hop-off bus tour.

Route Overview: From Place Royale, walk south along the ridge, popping into a stained-glass-filled Gothic church, and on to the best view of the city from the towering Palace of Justice. Then backtrack a bit and descend through the well-worn tapestries of the Sablon Quarter's antiques, art, and cafés, and down to the *Manneken-Pis* at the foot of the hill.

THE WALK BEGINS

❶ Place Royale

At the crest of the hill sits Place Royale, encircled by cars and trams and enclosed by white, Neoclassical buildings forming a mirror image around a cobblestone square. A big, green statue of a horseman stands in the center.

The statue—a Belgium-born Crusader, Godfrey de Bouillon (who led the First Crusade, in 1096)—rides forward carrying a flag, gazing down on the Town Hall spire. If Godfrey turned and looked left down Rue de la Régence, he'd see the domed Palace of Justice at the end of the boulevard. Over his right shoulder, just outside the square, is the Royal Palace, the king's residence.

In the 1800s, as Belgium exerted itself to industrialize and modernize, this area was rebuilt as a sign that Brussels had arrived as a world capital. Broad vistas down wide boulevards ending in gleaming white, Greek-columned monuments—the look was all the rage, seen in Paris, London, Washington, D.C....and here.

The cupola of the Church of St. Jacques sur Coudenberg—the central portion of the square's ring of buildings—makes the church look more like a bank building. But St. Jacques' church goes back much further than this building (from 1787); it originated in the 13th century near a 12th-century castle. Nobles chose to build their mansions in the neighborhood, and later, so did the king.

The Musical Instruments Museum is 30 yards downhill from the square, housed in an early-20th-century, iron-and-glass former department store. Its Art Nouveau facade was a deliberate attempt to get beyond the retro-looking Greek columns and domes of the Place Royale. Even if you don't visit the museum, you can ride the elevator up to the museum café for a superb Lower Town view.

• *Brussels' world-class Royal Museums of Fine Arts of Belgium are 30 yards south of Place Royale on Rue de la Régence. But before heading*

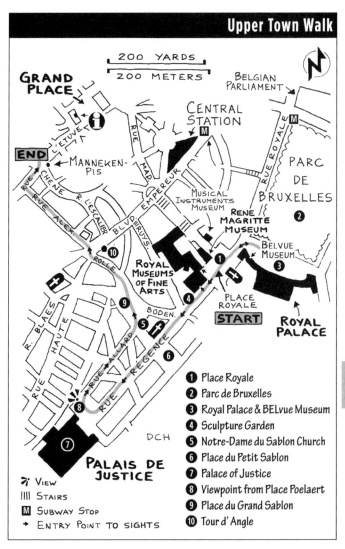

Upper Town Walk

200 YARDS
200 METERS

GRAND PLACE

BELGIAN PARLIAMENT

CENTRAL STATION
Ⓜ

END

MANNEKEN-PIS

RUE CHÊNE

R. LESCALIER

BLVD WRUYS.

BLVD EMPEREUR

RUE MAD.

MUSICAL INSTRUMENTS MUSEUM

RENE MAGRITTE MUSEUM

RUE ROYALE

PARC DE BRUXELLES

❷

RUE ALEX.

ROLLE

❿

ROYAL MUSEUMS OF FINE ARTS

BELVUE MUSEUM

❸

R. BLAES

RUE HAUTE

❾

BODEN.

❺

RUE ALLARD

RUE REGENCE

❻

❹

PLACE ROYALE

START

ROYAL PALACE

❽

DCH

❼

PALAIS DE JUSTICE

❶ Place Royale
❷ Parc de Bruxelles
❸ Royal Palace & BELvue Museum
❹ Sculpture Garden
❺ Notre-Dame du Sablon Church
❻ Place du Petit Sablon
❼ Palace of Justice
❽ Viewpoint from Place Poelaert
❾ Place du Grand Sablon
❿ Tour d'Angle

🛈 VIEW
||||| STAIRS
Ⓜ SUBWAY STOP
➤ ENTRY POINT TO SIGHTS

UPPER TOWN WALK

south, exit Place Royale on the north side (to the left as you face Godfrey),
which opens up to a large, tree-lined park.

❷ Parc de Bruxelles

Copying Versailles, the Habsburg empress Maria Theresa of
Austria (Marie-Antoinette's mom) had this symmetrical park
laid out in 1776, when she ruled (but never visited) the city. This is
just one of many large parks in Brussels, which expanded with an
awareness of the importance of city planning.

At the far (north) end of the park (directly opposite the Royal Palace, no need to actually walk there) is the Parliament building. Which parliament? The city hosts several—the European Parliament, the Belgian Parliament, and several local, city-council-type parliaments. This is the Belgian Parliament, often seen on nightly newscasts as a backdrop for the country's politicians.

In 1830, Belgian patriots rose up and converged on the park, where they attacked the troops of the Dutch king. This was the first blow in a short, almost blood-less revolution that drove out the foreign-born king and gave the Belgians independence...and a different foreign-born king.

• *The long building facing the park is the...*

❸ Royal Palace (Palais Royale)

After Belgium struck out twice trying to convince someone to be their new king, Leopold I (r. 1831–1865), a nobleman from Germany, agreed. Leopold was a steadying influence as the country modernized. His son rebuilt this palace—near the site of earlier palaces, dating back to the 10th century—by linking a row of townhouse mansions with a unifying facade (around 1870).

Leopold's great-great-great-grandnephew, King Albert II, today uses the palace as an office. (His head is on Belgium's euro coins.) Albert and his wife, Queen Paola, live in a palace north

of here (near the Atomium) and on the French Riviera. If the Belgian flag (black-yellow-red) is flying from the palace, the king is somewhere in Belgium.

Albert II (born 1932) is a figurehead king, as in so many European democracies, but he serves an important function as a common bond between bickering Flemish and Walloons. His son, Prince Philippe, is slated to succeed him, though Philippe—awkward and standoffish—is not as popular as his wife, Mathilde, also a Belgian native. Their little girl, Elisabeth, born in 2001, will become the first Belgian queen.

The bulk of the palace is off-limits to tourists except for six weeks in summer (palace generally open from the last week of July until the first week of Sept, gardens open April–May), but you can see an impressive exhibit on Belgian history and the royal family in the adjacent BELvue Museum.

• *Return to Place Royale, then continue south along Rue de la Régence, noticing the entrance to the Royal Museums of Fine Arts of Belgium. Just past the museums, on the right, you'll see a...*

❹ Sculpture Garden (Jardin de Sculpture)

This pleasant public garden—starring a statue by Rodin's contemporary, Aristide Maillol—looks like a great way to descend into the Sablon Quarter, but the gates at the bottom are often locked.

• *A hundred yards farther along, you reach the top of the Sablon neighborhood, dominated by the...*

❺ Notre-Dame du Sablon Church

The round, rose, stained-glass windows in the clerestory of this 14th-century Flamboyant Gothic church are nice by day, but are

thrilling at night, when the church is lit from inside. It glows like a lantern, enjoyed by locals at the cafés in the surrounding square.

Step inside. The glorious apse behind the altar—bathed in stained-glass light—is what Gothic is all about. Next to the altar, see a small wooden **statue of Mary** dressed in white with a lace veil. This is a copy,

made after iconoclastic Protestant vandals destroyed the original. The original statue was thought to have had miraculous powers that saved the town from plagues. In 1348, when the statue was in Antwerp, it spoke to a godly woman named Beatrix, prompting her to board a boat (see the small **wooden boat,** high above the entry door) and steal the statue away from Antwerp. When they tried to stop her, the Mary statue froze the Antwerp citizens in their tracks.

Beatrix and the statue arrived here, the Bruxelloise welcomed her with a joyous parade, and this large church was erected in her honor. Every summer, in Brussels' famous Ommegang, locals in tights and flamboyant costumes re-create the joyous arrival. With colorful banners and large puppets, they carry Mary from here through the city streets to the climax on the Grand Place.

• *On the other side of Rue de la Régence from the church is a leafy, fenced-off garden called the...*

❻ Place du Petit Sablon

This is a pleasant refuge from the busy street, part of why this neighborhood is considered so livable. The 48 small statues atop the wrought-iron fence represent the guilds—weavers, brewers, and butchers—of medieval Brussels. Inside the garden, 10 large statues represent hometown thinkers of the 16th century—a time of great intellectual accomplishments in Brussels. Gerardus Mercator (1512–1594), the Belgian mapmaker who devised a way

to show the spherical Earth on a flat surface, holds a globe.

• *We'll visit the Sablon neighborhood below the church later, but before losing elevation, let's continue along Rue de la Régence, passing the Music Academy and Brussels' main synagogue (its sidewalk fortified with concrete posts to keep car bombs at a distance), before reaching the long-scaffolded...*

❼ Palace of Justice (Palais de Justice)

This domed mountain of marble sits on the edge of the Upper Town ridge, dominating the Brussels skyline. Built in wedding-cake layers of Greek columns, it's topped with a dome taller than St. Peter's in Rome, rising 340 feet. Covering more than six acres, it's the size of a baseball stadium.

The palace was built in the time of King Leopold II (son of Leo I, r. 1865–1909) and epitomizes the brassy, look-at-me grandeur of his reign. Leopold became obscenely wealthy by turning Africa's Congo region—80 times the size of Belgium—into his personal colony. Whip-wielding Belgian masters forced African slaves to tend lucrative rubber plantations, exploiting the new craze for bicycle tires. Leopold spent much of this wealth expanding and beautifying the city of Brussels.

UPPER TOWN WALK

The building (which stands on the historic site of the town gallows) serves as a Hall of Justice, where major court cases are tried. If you pop into the lobby, you may see lawyers in black robes buzzing about.

• *On this square you'll notice a rack of city bikes. Like Paris, Brussels has a Cyclecity program that lets locals use bikes scattered all over town (note the map here) for a token €1 per hour. One of the best views of Brussels is immediately to the right of the Palace of Justice.*

❽ Viewpoint from Place Poelaert

You're standing 200 feet above the former Senne River Valley. Gazing west over the Lower Town, pan the valley from right (north) to left:

Near you is the stubby **clock tower** of the Minimen Church (which hosts lunchtime concerts in the summer). To the left of that, in the distance, past a tall square skyscraper, comes the lacy white Town Hall **spire** (marking the Grand Place).

In the far distance, six miles away, you can see one of the city's landmarks, the **Atomium.** (No doubt, someone atop it is looking back at you.) The Atomium's nine steel balls (all shiny after a 50th-anniversary restoration in 2008) form the shape of an iron molecule that is the size of the Palace of Justice behind you. Built for a 1958 World's Fair, it's now a middle-aged symbol of the dawn of the Atomic Era.

Next (closer to you) comes the **black-steepled roof** of the Notre-Dame de la Chapelle church, the city's oldest (from 1134, with a spire that starts Gothic and ends Baroque). On the distant horizon, see **five boxy skyscrapers,** part of the residential sprawl of this city of 1.8 million, which now covers 62 square miles. Breaking the horizon is a **green dome**—it belongs  to the Basilica of Koekelberg (fourth biggest in the world). And finally (panning quickly to the left), you see a **black glass skyscraper** marking the Midi (or South) train station, where you can catch the Eurostar to London.

At your feet lies the **Marolles neighborhood.** Once a funky, poor place where locals developed their own quirky dialogue, it remains somewhat seedy—and famous for its sprawling flea market (daily 7:00–14:00, best on weekends). Two of the streets just below you—Rue Haute and Rue Blaes—are lined with secondhand shops. An **elevator** connects Place Poelaert with the Marolles neighborhood (free, daily 6:00–23:00). People who brake for garage sales may want to cut out of this walk early and head to the Marolles from here.

Gazing off into the distance to the far left (south), you can't quite see the suburb of **Waterloo,** 10 miles away. But try to imagine it, because it was there that the tide of European history turned. On the morning of June 18, 1815, Napoleon waited two hours for the ground to dry before sending his troops into battle. That delay may have cost him the battle. His 72,000 soldiers could have defeated Wellington's 68,000, but the two-hour delay was just enough time for Wellington's reinforcements to arrive—45,000 Prussian troops. Napoleon had to surrender, his rule of Europe ended, and Belgium was placed under a Dutch king—until the Belgians won their independence in the 1830 revolution.

Behind you, in Place Poelaert, are two memorials to the two World Wars, both of which passed through Belgium with deadly force.

• *Backtrack east, descending to Place du Grand Sablon by walking down Rue Ernest Allard.*

❾ Place du Grand Sablon

The Sablon neighborhood features cafés and restaurants, antiques

stores, and art galleries. Chocolatier Wittamer (on the far side of the square, at #6) often has elaborate window displays. Every weekend, there's an antiques market on the square. On warm summer evenings, the square sparks magic, as sophisticated locals sip apéritifs at the café tables, admiring the glowing stained glass of the church.

• *Sloping Place du Grand Sablon funnels downhill into the pedestrian-only street called Rue de Rollebeek, which leads past fun shops to the busy Boulevard de l'Empereur. To the right on the boulevard, just past the bowling alley, is the...*

❿ Tour d'Angle

The "Corner Tower" is a rare surviving section of Brussels' 13th-century city wall, and was one of seven gates along the 2.5-mile-long wall that enclosed Brussels, one of Europe's great cities.

• *The Central Train station is two blocks directly ahead. Or continue downhill several blocks, and when you hit level ground, turn right on Rue L'Etuve, which leads directly back to the Grand Place. A block along, you'll run into our old friend* Manneken-Pis, *eternally relieving himself.*

ROYAL MUSEUMS OF FINE ARTS OF BELGIUM TOUR

Musées Royaux des Beaux-Arts de Belgique

Two large buildings, each housing an art museum (ancient and modern), contain a vast collection covering the entire history of Western painting. The collection, while enjoyable, can be overwhelming, so this chapter gives a tour of a "Top 10" list highlighting the Ancient Art and Modern Art museums' strengths: Flemish and Belgian artists. In June of 2009, the complex will expand with the new Magritte Museum, celebrating the work of the popular Belgian Surrealist with over 150 statues, paintings, and drawings.

ORIENTATION

Cost: €5 for Ancient Art and Modern Art museums; €8 for Magritte Museum.

Hours: Ancient Art and Modern Art museums—Tue–Sun 10:00–17:00, closed Mon, last entry at 16:30; Magritte Museum Tue–Sun 9:30–17:00, Wed until 20:00, closed Mon.

Getting There: The museums are at Rue de la Régence 3 in the Upper Town, just a five-minute walk uphill from Central Station (or take bus #20, #38, #71, or #95; or tram #92 or #94). You'll also encounter the museums if you take my Upper Town Walk.

Information: Consider the excellent €2.50 audioguide or the €2.50 tour booklet (*Twenty Masterpieces of the Art of Painting: A Brief Guided Tour*, sold in the museum shop). You can also choose among four self-guided tours, each marked with a different color: blue for the 15th and 16th centuries, brown for the 17th and 18th, and green for the 20th. Tel. 02-508-3211, www.fine-arts-museum.be.

Length of This Tour: Allow one hour.

Cuisine Art: The Greshem, a restaurant and tea room, is nearby at Place Royale (daily 11:00–18:00). The museums also have a crummy café and a fancy brasserie on-site.

Overview

There are technically three museums here: the Ancient Art (pre-1800) and Modern Art (post-1800) museums are connected via a labyrinthine series of passageways. The museum complex sprawls over several wings and a dozen floors, and to see it all is a logistical nightmare. Your first stop should be the information desk, which has the latest on renovations, room closings, and the new Magritte Museum (located nearby in a separate building). Armed with the museum's free map (supplemented with the audioguide), make your way through the maze to find these 10 highlights.

THE TOUR BEGINS

• *Start with the Flemish masters, one floor up in the Ancient Art Museum, and follow the blue tour signs. In Room 11, you'll find...*

ANCIENT ART

Rogier van der Weyden (c. 1399–1464)—*Portrait of Anthony of Burgundy (Portrait d' Antoine de Bourgogne)*

Anthony was known in his day as the Great Bastard, the bravest and most distinguished of the many bastards fathered by prolific Duke Philip the Good (a Renaissance prince whose sense of style impressed Florence's young Lorenzo the Magnificent, patron of the arts).

Anthony, a member of the Archers Guild, fingers the arrow like a bow-string. From his gold necklace dangles a Golden Fleece, one of Europe's more prestigious knightly honors. Wearing a black cloak, a bowl-cut hairdo, and a dark-red cap, with his pale face and hand emerging from a dark background, the man who'd been called a bastard all his life gazes to the distance, his clear, sad eyes lit with a speckle of white paint.

Van der Weyden, Brussels' official portrait painter, faithfully rendered life-size, lifelike portraits of wealthy traders, bankers, and craftsmen. Here he captures the wrinkles in Anthony's neck, and the faint shadow his chin casts on his Adam's apple. Van der Weyden had also painted Philip the Good (in Bruges' Groeninge

Museum), and young Anthony's long, elegant face and full lips are a mirror image—pretty convincing DNA evidence in a paternity suit.

Capitalist Flanders in the 1400s was one of the richest, most cultured, and progressive areas in Europe, rivaling Florence and Venice.

• *In Room 14, find...*

Hans Memling (c. 1430-1494)—*Martyrdom of St. Sebastian (Volets d'un Triptyque)*

Serene Sebastian is filled with arrows by a serene firing squad in a serene landscape. Sebastian, a Roman captain who'd converted to Christianity, was ordered to be shot to death. (He miraculously survived, so they clubbed him to death.)

Ready, freeze! Like a *tableaux vivant* (popular with Philip the Good's crowd), the well-dressed archers and saint freeze this moment in the martyrdom so the crowd can applaud the colorful costumes and painted cityscape backdrop.

Hans Memling, along with his former employer, Rogier van der Weyden, are called Flemish Primitives. Why "Primitive"? For the lack of 3-D realism so admired in Italy at the time (for more on Flemish Primitives, see sidebar). Sebastian's arm is tied to a branch that's not arching overhead, as it should be, but instead is behind him. An archer aims slightly behind, not at, Sebastian. The other archer strings his bow in a stilted pose. But Memling is clearly a master of detail, and the faces, beautiful textiles, and hazy landscape combine to create a meditative mood appropriate to the church altar in Bruges where this painting was once placed.

• *In Room 31, look for...*

Pieter Brueghel I, the Elder (c. 1527-1569)—*The Census at Bethlehem*

Perched at treetop level, you have a bird's-eye view over a snow-covered village near Brussels. The canals are frozen over, but life goes on, with everyone doing something. Kids throw snowballs and sled across the ice. A crowd gathers at the inn (lower left), where a woman holds a pan to catch blood while a man slaughters a pig. Most everyone has his or her back to us or head covered, so the figures speak through poses and motions.

Into the scene rides a woman on a donkey led by a man—it's Mary and husband Joseph hoping to find a room at the inn (or at

ROYAL MUSEUMS TOUR

least a manger), because Mary's going into labor.

The year is 1566—the same year that Protestant extremists throughout the Low Countries vandalized Catholic churches, tearing down "idolatrous" statues and paintings of the Virgin Mary. Brueghel (more discreetly) brings Mary down to earth from her Triumphant Coronation in heaven, and places Jesus' birth in the humble here and now. The busy villagers put their heads down and work, oblivious to the future Mother of God and the wonder about to take place.

Brueghel the Elder was famous for his landscapes filled with crowds of peasants in motion. His religious paintings place the miraculous in everyday settings.

In this room, you'll see Brueghel's works, as well as those of his less-famous sons. Pieter Brueghel II, the younger Pieter, copied dad's style (and even some paintings, like the *Census at Bethlehem*). Another son, Jan, was known as the "Velvet Brueghel" for his glossy still lifes of flower arrangements.

• *Leave the blue tour and walk through to Room 34 and beyond, to the main hallway in this wing, in order to follow the brown tour signs. You'll find lots of Rubens in Rooms 52 and 53, including the wallsized...*

Peter Paul Rubens (1577-1640)—*The Ascent to Calvary (La Montée au Calvaire)*

Life-size figures scale this 18-foot-tall canvas on the way to Christ's Crucifixion. The scene ripples with motion, from the windblown clothes to steroid-enhanced muscles to billowing flags and a troubled sky. Christ stumbles, and might get trampled by the surging crowd. Veronica kneels to gently wipe his bloody head.

This 200-square-foot canvas was manufactured by Rubens at his studio in Antwerp. Hiring top-notch assistants, Rubens could crank out large altarpieces for the area's Catholic churches. First, Rubens himself did a small-scale sketch in oil (like many of the studies in Room 52). He would then make other sketches, highlighting individual details. His assistants would reproduce them on the large canvas, and Rubens would then add the final touches.

This work is from late in Rubens' long and very successful career. He got a second wind in his 50s, when he married 16-year-old Hélène Fourment. She was the model for Veronica, who consoles the faltering Christ in this painting.

• *To get to the Modern Art wing, return to the ground floor and the large main entrance hall of the Ancient Museum. From there, a passageway leads to the Modern Art Museum. Once in the Modern Art wing (entering on Level −3), take the elevator—which is so slow, they actually provide chairs inside the elevator itself—down to the lowest level (−8), filled with paintings from the 19th and 20th centuries. Work your way back up, keeping an eye out for the paintings described below. Enlist the help of nearby guards if you can't find any of these pieces.*

MODERN ART

• *Watch Impressionism turn to Post-Impressionism in this wing, which features both. Paul Gauguin and Georges Seurat emerged from Paris' Impressionist community to forge their own styles. Begin by visiting with...*

Georges Seurat (1859–1891)—*The Seine at Grand-Jatte* (*La Seine à la Grande-Jatte*, 1888)

Seurat paints a Sunday-in-the-park view from his favorite island in the Seine. Taking Impressionism to its extreme, he builds the scene out of small points of primary colors that blend at a distance to form objects. The bright colors capture the dazzling, sunlit atmosphere of this hazy day.

Paul Gauguin (1848–1903)—*Breton Calvary* (*Calvaire Breton*, 1889; a.k.a. *The Green Christ/Le Christ Vert*)

Paul Gauguin returned to the bold, black, coloring-book outlines of more Primitive (pre-3-D) art. The Christian statue and countryside look less like Brittany and more like primitive Tahiti, where Gauguin would soon settle.

James Ensor (1860–1949)—*Shocked Masks* (*1883*)

At 22, James Ensor, an acclaimed child prodigy, proudly presented his lively Impressionist-style works to the Brussels Salon

ROYAL MUSEUMS TOUR

for exhibition. They were flatly rejected.

The artist withdrew from public view and, in seclusion, painted *Shocked Masks,* a dark and murky scene set in a small room of an ordinary couple wearing grotesque masks. Once again, everyone disliked this disturbing canvas and heaped more criticism on him. For the next six decades, Ensor painted the world as he saw it—full of bizarre, carnival-masked, stupid-looking crowds of cruel strangers who mock the viewer.

Jacques-Louis David (1748–1825)—*The Death of Marat* (1793)

In a scene ripped from the day's headlines, Marat—a well-known crusading French journalist—has been stabbed to death in his

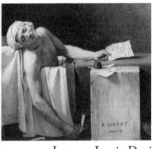

bathtub by Charlotte Corday, a conservative fanatic. Marat's life drains out of him, turning the bathwater red. With his last strength, he pens a final, patriotic, *"Vive la Révolution"* message to his fellow patriots. Corday, a young noblewoman angered by Marat's campaign to behead the French king, was arrested and guillotined three days later.

Jacques-Louis David, one of Marat's fellow revolutionaries, set to work painting a tribute to his fallen comrade. (He signed the painting: *"À Marat"*—"To Marat.")

David makes it a secular *pietà,* with the brave writer as a martyred Christ in a classic dangling-arm pose. Still, the deathly pallor and harsh lighting pull no punches, creating in-your-face realism.

David, the official art director of the French Revolution, supervised propaganda and the costumes worn for patriotic parades. A year later (1794), his extreme brand of revolution (which included guillotining thousands of supposed enemies) was squelched by moderates, and David was jailed. He emerged again as Napoleon's court painter. When Napoleon was exiled in 1815, so was David, spending his last years in Brussels.

Paul Delvaux (1897–1994)

Delvaux, who studied, worked, and taught in Brussels, became famous for his surrealistic paintings of nude women, often wandering through weirdly lit landscapes. They cast long shadows, wandering bare-breasted among classical ruins. Some women grow roots.

• *Along with other Surrealist artists represented in this museum, such as Joan Miró, Salvador Dalí, Max Ernst, Yves Tanguy, and Roberto Matta, you'll see plenty of paintings by Magritte in the new René Magritte Museum.*

René Magritte (1898–1967)

Magritte paints real objects with photographic clarity, then jumbles them together in new and provocative ways.

Magritte had his own private reserve of symbolic images. You'll see clouds, blue sky, windows, the female torso, men in bowler hats, rocks, and castles arranged side by side as if they should mean something. People morph into animals or inanimate objects. The juxtaposition short-circuits your brain only when you try to make sense of it.

Magritte also trained and worked in Brussels. Though he's world-famous now, it took decades before his peculiar brand of Surrealism caught on.

SLEEPING

Normal hotel prices are high in central Brussels. But if you arrive in July, August, or on a Friday or Saturday night any other time, the city's fancy business-class hotels rent rooms for half price, making them your best budget bet. Otherwise, you do have budget options. The modern hostels are especially good and rent double rooms. April, May, September, and October are very crowded, and finding a room without a reservation can be impossible.

Business Hotels with Summer Rates

The fancy hotels of Brussels (Db-€150–200) survive because of the business and diplomatic trade. But they're desperately empty in July and August (sometimes June, too) and on weekends (most Fri, Sat, and—to a lesser extent—Sun nights). Ask for a summer/weekend rate and you'll save about a third. If you go through the TI, you'll save up to two-thirds. Three-star hotels in the center abound with amazing summer rates—you can rent a double room with enough comforts to keep a diplomat happy, including a fancy breakfast, for about €60.

The TI assures me that every day in July and August, tons of business-class hotel rooms are on the push list; you'll get a big discount just by showing up at either TI (for same-day booking only). In July and August and on any Friday or Saturday—trust me—your best value is to arrive without a reservation, walk from the Central Station down to either TI, and let them book you a room within a few blocks. You cannot book these deals in advance. They are only for the bold who show up without a reservation. The later you arrive, the lower the prices drop (room-booking TI closes at 19:00 July–Aug, last booking at 18:30).

If you're nervous about traveling without advance reservations, contact the TI by email (info@visitflanders.be) and ask which

Sleep Code

(€1 = about $1.40, country code: 32)
S = Single, **D** = Double/Twin, **T** = Triple, **Q** = Quad, **b** = bathroom,
s = shower only. Everyone speaks English and accepts credit
cards. Unless otherwise noted, breakfast is included.
       To help you easily sort through these listings, I've divided
the rooms into three categories, based on the price for a
standard double room with bath:

$$$ Higher Priced—Most rooms €100 or more.
 $$ Moderately Priced—Most rooms between €80–100.
  $ Lower Priced—Most rooms €80 or less.

business-class hotels will have special rates during your visit. Ask
for the cheapest three-star place near the Grand Place. Historically
the Hotel Ibis Centre Ste. Catherine has double rooms with bath
and breakfast for €50 through the summer.

These seasonal rates apply only to business-class hotels.
Because of this, budget accommodations, which charge the
same throughout the year, go from being a good value one day
(say, a Thursday in October) to a bad value the next (a Friday in
October).

Hotels near the Grand Place

$$$ Hotel Ibis off Grand Place is well-situated halfway between
the Central Station and the Grand Place, the best of six Ibis
locations in or near Brussels. It's a sprawling, modern hotel offer-
ing 184 quiet, simple, industrial-strength-yet-comfy rooms (Sb/
Db-€145 Mon–Thu, €90–100 Fri–Sun and daily July–Aug, extra
bed-€20, breakfast-€13, non-smoking rooms, air-con, elevator,
Grasmarkt 100, tel. 02-514-1223, fax 02-514-5067, www.ibishotel
.com, h1046@accor.com).

$$$ Hotel Le Dixseptième, a four-star luxury hotel ide-
ally located a block below Central Station, is an expensive oasis
in the heart of town. Prim, proper, and peaceful, with chande-
liers and squeaky hardwood floors, its 24 rooms come with all the
comforts. Each is decorated with a different theme (Db-€200,
Db suites-€270, extra bed-€30, 25 percent off Fri–Sat and daily
July–Aug, see website for discounts, air-con, elevator, Rue de
la Madeleine 25, tel. 02-517-1717, fax 02-502-6424, www.ledix
septieme.be, info@ledixseptieme.be).

$$$ Hotel La Madeleine, on the small square between
Central Station and the Grand Place, rents 55 plain, dimly lit
rooms. It has a great location and a friendly staff (S-€55; Ss-€78,

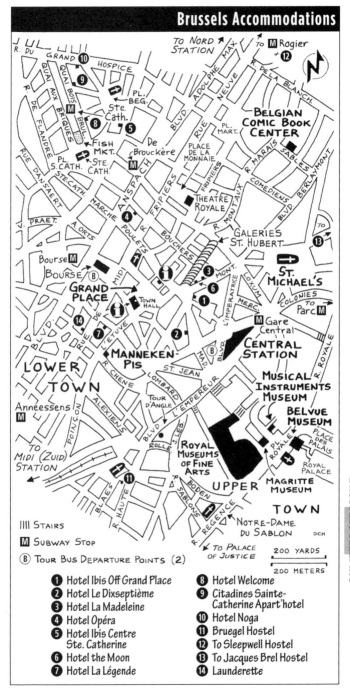

Brussels Accommodations

TO NORD STATION

TO M Rogier

R. DU GRAND HOSPICE

QUAI BOIS

QUAI AUX BRIQUES

PL. BEG.

Ste. Cath.

FISH MKT.

De Brouckère

PL. S. CATH.

Ste. CATH.

RUE DANSAERT

MARCHE

PRAET.

A. ORTS

ADOLPHE MAX

NEUVE

R. DE LA BLANCH.

PL. MART.

PLACE DE LA MONNAIE

FRIPIERS

RUE MARAIS

COMEDIENS

BLVD. BERLAYMONT

SABLE.

BELGIAN COMIC BOOK CENTER

THEATRE ROYALE

GALERIES ST. HUBERT

R. MONTAUX

Bourse M

BOURSE B

GRAND PLACE

TOWN HALL

MANNEKEN-PIS

LETUVE

MONT.

L'IMPERATRICE

LOXUM

MERCI.

LOXUM

COLONIES

ST. MICHAEL'S

TO Parc M

M Gare Central

CENTRAL STATION

LOWER TOWN

Annéessens M

TO MIDI (ZUID) STATION

R. CHENE

ST. JEAN

TOUR D'ANGLE

ALEXIENS

LOMBARD

L'EMPEREUR

MAD.

BLVD.

J. LEB.

ROLLE

ROYAL MUSEUMS OF FINE ARTS

MUSICAL INSTRUMENTS MUSEUM

BELVUE MUSEUM

PLACE DES PALAIS

PL. ROYALE

ROYAL PALACE

MAGRITTE MUSEUM

UPPER TOWN

R. HAUTE

BLAES

BODEN

R. SABLONS

REGENCE

R. ROYALE

NOTRE-DAME DU SABLON

TO PALACE OF JUSTICE

200 YARDS

200 METERS

IIII STAIRS

M SUBWAY STOP

B TOUR BUS DEPARTURE POINTS (2)

1 Hotel Ibis Off Grand Place
2 Hotel Le Dixseptième
3 Hotel La Madeleine
4 Hotel Opéra
5 Hotel Ibis Centre Ste. Catherine
6 Hotel the Moon
7 Hotel La Légende

8 Hotel Welcome
9 Citadines Sainte-Catherine Apart'hotel
10 Hotel Noga
11 Bruegel Hostel
12 To Sleepwell Hostel
13 To Jacques Brel Hostel
14 Launderette

Sb-€102, Db-€112; "executive" rooms: Sb-€122, Db-€127, Tb-€137; 20 percent off Fri–Sat, 30 percent off July–Aug—see website for deals; family room for four available, request a quieter back room when you reserve, elevator, Wi-Fi, Rue de la Montagne 22, tel. 02-513-2973, fax 02-502-1350, www.hotel-la-madeleine.be, info @hotel-la-madeleine.be, Philippe).

$$$ Hotel Opéra, on a great, people-filled street near the Grand Place, is professional but standardized, with lots of street noise and 49 well-worn rooms (Sb-€82, Db-€105 or €85 in July–Aug, Tb-€135, Qb-€150, 10 percent less with this book in 2009, request quieter courtyard rooms, elevator, Wi-Fi, Rue Gretry 53, tel. 02-219-4343, fax 02-219-1720, www.hotel-opera.be, reception @hotel-opera.be).

$$ Hotel Ibis Centre Ste. Catherine is a big, impersonal, perfectly comfortable place with a great location that offers very deep discounts during its slow times only via the TI. Its double rooms, which are reasonable all year (Db-€80–100) rent for €50 with breakfast through the summer only when booked through the TI (Rue Joseph Plateau Straat 2 at Place Ste. Catherine, tel. 02-513-7620, fax 02-514-2214, www.ibishotel.com, h1454 @accor.com).

$$ Hotel the Moon is concrete and efficient, with 17 fresh, industrial-strength rooms and no public spaces. Although it has absolutely no character, you'll sleep fine and it's super–convenient, right in the old center (Sb-€50–70, Db-€60–90, Tb-€75–120, lower prices are for July–Aug, 10 percent discount with this book in 2009, Rue de la Montagne 4, tel. 02-508-1580, fax 02-508-1585, www.memon-hotels.be, info@hotelthemoon.com).

$$ Hotel La Légende rents 26 rooms with a dormitory ambience a block from the *Manneken-Pis* statue. Although it's on a busy road, it has a pleasant courtyard. The furnishings are basic, but the location and price are right and the rooms are comfortable enough (standard Db-€95, newer Db-€120, Tb-€145, Qb-€155, 30 percent off on weekends and July–Aug, elevator, Rue du Lombard 35, tel. 02-512-8290, fax 02-512-3493, www.hotellalegende.com, info @hotellalegende.com).

Hotels Around the Fish Market

The next three listings are a 10-minute walk from the intensity of the old center, near the Ste. Catherine Métro stop. This charming neighborhood, called "the village in Brussels," faces the canalside fish market and has many of the town's best restaurants.

$$$ Hotel Welcome, owned by an energetic bundle of hospitality named Meester Smeester, offers outrageously creative rooms, exuberantly decorated with artifacts he's picked up in his world travels. Each of the 16 rooms has a different geographic theme—

from India to Japan to Bali (Sb-€95, standard Db-€120, deluxe Db-€140, large suite-€210, much lower rates in Aug, special 20 percent off—even on discounted rates—with two-night stay and this book, elevator, Internet access and Wi-Fi, parking-€10, airport shuttle available, 23 Quai au Bois à Brûler, tel. 02-219-9546, fax 02-217-1887, www.brusselshotel.travel, info@hotelwelcome.com, run by Sophie and Michel Smeesters, plus Vincent and Natasha). Tour Michel's rooms on the Web.

$$$ Citadines Sainte-Catherine Apart'hotel, part of a Europe-wide chain, is a huge apartment-style hotel with modern, shipshape rooms. Choose from efficiency studios with fold-out double beds or two-room apartments with a bedroom and a fold-out couch in the living room. All 163 units come with a kitchen, stocked cupboards, a stereo, and everything you need to settle right in (one- or two-person studio-€125, €63 July–Aug; apartment for up to four people-€155, €105 July–Aug; 15 percent cheaper by the week, breakfast-€13, Wi-Fi, parking-€10, 51 Quai au Bois à Brûler, tel. 02-221-1411, fax 02-221-1599, www.citadines.com, stecatherine@citadines.com).

$$$ Hotel Noga feels extremely homey, with 19 rooms, a welcoming game room, and old photos of Belgian royalty lining the hallways. It's carefully run by Frederich Faucher and his son, Mourad (Sb-€90, Db-€110, Tb-€135, Qb-€160, all rooms about 20 percent off Fri–Sat and in Aug, 5 percent discount if you pay in cash, very quiet, non-smoking rooms, Rue du Beguinage 38, tel. 02-218-6763, fax 02-218-1603, www.nogahotel.com, info@noga hotel.com).

Hostels

Three classy and modern hostels—in buildings that could double as small, state-of-the-art, minimum-security prisons—are within a 10-minute walk of the Central Station. Each accepts people of all ages, serves cheap and hot meals, takes credit cards, and charges about the same price. All rates include breakfast and showers down the hall.

$ Bruegel Hostel, a fortress of cleanliness, is handiest and most comfortable. Of its many rooms, 22 are bunk-bed doubles (S-€31, D-€45, beds in quads or dorms-€18.60, nonmembers pay €3 extra per night, includes sheets and breakfast, open 7:00–13:00 & 14:00–1:00 in the morning, Rue de St. Esprit 2 midway between Midi and Central stations, behind Chapelle church, tel. 02-511-0436, fax 02-512-0711, www.vjh.be, brussel@vjh.be).

$ Sleepwell, surrounded by high-rise parking structures, is also comfortable (S-€41, D-€60, T-€85, dorm beds-€19–30, reduced rates for multi-night stays, includes breakfast, non-smoking, Internet access in lobby, Rue de Damier 23, tel. 02-218-5050, fax 02-218-1313, www.sleepwell.be, info@sleepwell.be).

$ Jacques Brel is a little farther out, but it's still a reasonable walk from everything (171 beds, S-€32, D-€46, dorm bed-€16–18, includes breakfast and sheets, no curfew, non-smoking rooms, laundry, Rue de la Sablonnière 30, tel. 02-218-0187, fax 02-217-2005, www.laj.be, brussels.brel@laj.be).

EATING

For many, the obvious eating tip in Brussels is simply to enjoy the Grand Place. My vote for northern Europe's grandest medieval square is lined with hardworking eateries that serve the predictable dishes to tourist crowds. Of course, you won't get the best quality or prices—but, after all, it's the Grand Place. Locals advise eating well elsewhere and enjoying a Grand Place perch for dessert or a drink. While many tourists congregate at the Rue des Bouchers, "Restaurant Row," consider a wander through the new emerging eating zone—gay, ethnic, and trendy—past the Bourse near Place Saint-Géry. Compare the ambience, check posted menus, and choose your favorite.

Brussels is known for both its high-quality, French-style cuisine and for multicultural variety. Seafood—fish, eel, shrimp, and oysters—is especially well-prepared here. As in France, if you ask for the *menu* (muh-noo) at a restaurant, you won't get a list of dishes; you'll get a fixed-price meal. *Menus*, which include three or four courses, are generally a good value if you're hungry. Ask for *la carte* (lah kart) if you want to see a printed menu and order à la carte, like the locals do.

Mussels in Brussels

Mussels *(moules)* are available all over town. For an atmospheric cellar or a table right on the Grand Place, eat at **'t Kelderke.** Its one steamy vault under the square is always packed with both natives and tourists—a real Brussels fixture. It serves local specialties, including mussels (a splittable kilo bucket—just more than 2 pounds—for €20–22; daily 12:00–24:00, Thu–Sat until 2:00 in the morning, no reservations, Grand Place 15, tel. 02-513-7344). Also see Restaurant Chez Leon, next page.

Rue des Bouchers ("Restaurant Row")

Brussels' restaurant streets, two blocks north of the Grand Place, are touristy and notorious for aggressively sucking you in and ripping you off. But the area is an exhilarating spectacle and fun for at least a walk. Order carefully, understand the prices thoroughly, and watch your wallet.

Restaurant Chez Leon is a touristy mussels factory, slamming out piles of good, cheap buckets since 1893. It's big and welcoming, with busy green-aproned waiters offering a "Formula Leon" for €14.50—a light meal consisting of a small bucket of mussels, fries, and a beer. They also offer a €28.50 fixed-price meal that comes with a starter, a large bucket of mussels, fries, and beer (daily 12:00–23:00, kids under 12 eat free, Rue des Bouchers 18, tel. 02-511-1415). In the family portrait of Leon's brother Honoré (hanging in the corner), the wife actually looks like a mussel.

Aux Armes de Bruxelles is a venerable restaurant that has been serving reliably good food to locals in a dressy setting for generations. This is another food factory, with white-suited waiters serving an older clientele impressed by the restaurant's reputation. You'll pay a bit more for the formality (€24 fixed-price lunch, €35–46 fixed-price dinner, Tue–Sun 12:00–23:00, closed Mon, indoor seating only, Rue des Bouchers 13, tel. 02-511-5550).

Restaurant Vincent has you enter through the kitchen to enjoy their 1905-era ambience (€27.50 fixed-price meal, Mon–Sat 12:00–14:30 & 18:30–23:00, Sun 12:00–15:00 & 18:30–22:30, Rue des Dominicains 8–10, tel. 02-511-2607, Michel and Jacques).

Finer Dining

Restaurant de l'Ogenblik, a remarkably peaceful eddy just off the raging restaurant row, fills an early-20th-century space in the corner of an arcade. The dressy waiters serve well-presented, near-gourmet French cuisine (€24–27 plates, Mon–Sat 12:00–14:30 & 19:00–24:00, closed Sun, across from Restaurant Vincent—listed above—at Galerie des Princes 1, tel. 02-511-6151, Yves). A mussels-free zone, their rack of lamb with 10 vegetables is great.

Belga Queen Brasserie bills itself as a "wonderfood place." A huge, trendy, dressy brasserie filling a palatial former bank building, it's *the* spot for Brussels' beautiful people and visiting European diplomats. While a little more expensive than the alternatives, the "creative Belgian cuisine" is excellent, the service is sharp, and the experience is memorable—from the fries served in silver cones, to the double-decker platters of iced shellfish, to the transparent toilets stalls (which become opaque only after you nervously lock the door). The high-powered trendiness can make you feel a little gawky, but if you've got the money, this is a great splurge. Consider their €33 three-course, fixed-price meal with

Brussels Restaurants

1. 't Kelderke
2. Restaurant Chez Leon
3. Aux Armes de Bruxelles
4. Rest. Vincent & de l'Ogenblik
5. Belga Queen Brasserie
6. Le Mokafé
7. La Maison des Crêpes
8. Osteria a l'Ombra
9. Pitta Creta Grill
10. Panos Sandwiches
11. AD Delhaize Grocery
12. Super GB Grocery
13. Bij den Boer & Rest. Jacques
14. La Marie Joseph
15. Restaurant La Marée
16. Restaurant Le Pré Salé
17. La Villette Restaurant
18. A la Mort Subite Bar
19. Le Cirio Café
20. A la Bécasse Café
21. Fin de Siècle & Le Greenwich Bars

matching beers (€20–30 entrées, €30–42 fixed-price meals, daily 12:00–14:30 & 19:00–24:00, call to reserve, two seatings: about 19:30 and 21:30, Rue Fosse-aux-Loups 32, tel. 02-217-2187). The vault downstairs is a plush cigar and cocktail lounge. For just a drink, grab a stool at the white-marble oyster bar.

More Eateries near the Grand Place

Le Mokafé is inexpensive but feels splurgy. It's in the quiet end of the elegant Galeries St. Hubert with great people-watching outdoor tables (€8 spaghetti, €10 salads, daily 8:00–24:00, Galerie du Roi 9, tel. 02-511-7870).

La Maison des Crêpes, a little eatery half a block south of the Bourse, looks underwhelming but serves delicious €8–10 crêpes (savory and sweet) and salads. It has a brown café ambience, and even though it's just a few steps away from the tourist bustle, it feels laid-back and local (good beers, fresh mint tea, sidewalk seating, daily 12:00–23:00, Rue du Midi 13).

Osteria a l'Ombra, a true Italian joint, is perfect for anyone needing a quality bowl of pasta with a fine glass of Italian wine. Across the lane from the TI and just a block off the Grand Place, it's pricey, but the woody bistro ambience and tasty food make it a good value. If you choose an entrée (about €15), your choice of pasta or salad is included in the price. While the ground-floor seating is fine, also consider sitting upstairs (Mon–Fri 12:00–15:00 & 18:30–23:30, Sat 18:30–23:30, closed Sun, Rue des Harengs 2, tel. 02-511-6710).

Cheap Eats on Grasmarkt: The Grasmarkt is lined with low-end eateries, especially fun on sunny days. To eat for less here, check out the **Pitta Creta Grill** (€3–4 pita sandwiches) or the **Panos** sandwich place.

Groceries: Two supermarkets are about a block from the Bourse and a few blocks from the Grand Place. **AD Delhaize** is at the intersection of Anspach and Marché-aux-Poulets (Mon–Sat 9:00–20:00, Fri until 21:00, Sun 9:00–18:00), and **Super GB** is half a block away at Halles and Marché-aux-Poulets (Mon–Sat 9:00–20:00, Fri until 21:00, closed Sun). **Mini-Markets** dot the city. Generally run by Pakistani and Indian immigrants, they are expensive but handy (open very late, drinks, groceries, phone cards).

Around the Sainte Catherine Fish Market

A 10-minute walk from the old center puts you in "the village within the city" area of Sainte Catherine (Métro: Ste. Catherine). The historic fish market here has spawned a tradition of fine restaurants specializing mostly in seafood. The old fish canal survives, and if you walk around it, you'll see plenty of enticing restaurants.

Make the circuit, considering these very good yet very different eating options.

Bij den Boer, a fun, noisy eatery popular with locals and tourists, feels like a traditional and very successful brasserie. The specialty: fish (€30 four-course fixed-price meal, Mon–Sat 12:00–14:30 & 18:00–22:30, closed Sun, Quai aux Briques 60, tel. 02-512-6122). Its neighbor, **Restaurant Jacques** (at #44, tel. 02-513-2762), also has a good reputation. You'll start things off with a free bowl of little gray shrimp as an appetizer.

La Marie Joseph, stylish and modern—both the food and the clientele—serves fancy fish and fries and earns raves from the natives (€25 plates, Tue–Sun 12:00–15:00 & 18:30–23:00, closed Mon, no reservations, Quai au Bois à Brûler 47, tel. 02-218-0596).

Restaurant La Marée is a classic local scene a couple of blocks away from the trendy canalside places. A non-touristy bistro with an open kitchen and an inviting menu, it specializes in mussels and seafood (closed Sun–Mon, near Rue du Marché aux Porcs at Rue de Flandre 99, tel. 02-511-0040).

Restaurant Le Pré Salé is noisy, high-energy, and family-friendly. A Brussels fixture for its traditional local cuisine, it fills a former butcher shop with happy eaters and a busy open kitchen (big, shareable €21 pots of mussels come with a salad, €15 meals, Wed–Sun 12:00–14:30 & 18:30–22:30, closed Mon–Tue, a block off the fish market at Rue de Flandre 20, tel. 02-513-6545).

La Villette Restaurant is a romantic, low-energy, seafood-free alternative, serving traditional Belgian cuisine: heavy, meaty stews and dishes with beer. It has a charming red-and-white-table-cloth interior and good outdoor seating facing a small square (€14 two-course fixed-price lunch, €15–18 meals, Mon–Fri 12:00–14:30 & 18:30–22:30, Sat 18:30–22:30 only, closed Sun, Rue du Vieux Marché-aux-Grains 3, tel. 02-512-7550, Agata).

Sampling Belgian Beer with Food and Ambience

Looking for a good spot to enjoy that famous Belgian beer? Brussels is full of atmospheric cafés to savor the local brew. The eateries lining the Grand Place are touristy, but the setting—plush old medieval guild halls fronting all that cobbled wonder—is hard to beat. I've listed three places a few minutes' walk off the square, all with a magical, old-time feel. If you'd like something to wash down with your beer, you can generally get a cold-meat plate, an open-face sandwich, or a salad.

All varieties of Belgian beer are available, but Brussels' most distinctive beers are *lambic*-based. Look for *lambic doux, lambic blanche, gueuze* (pronounced "kurrs"), and *faro*, as well as fruit-flavored *lambics*, such as *kriek* (cherry) and *framboise* (raspberry—

frambozen in Flemish). These beers look and taste more like a dry, somewhat bitter cider. The brewer doesn't add yeast—the beer ferments naturally from yeast found floating only in the marshy air around Brussels.

A la Mort Subite, north of the restaurant streets, is a classic old bar that has retained its 1928 decor...and many of its 1928 customers (Mon–Sat 11:00–24:00, Sun 13:00–22:00, Rue Montagne-aux-Herbes Potagères 7, tel. 02-513-1318). Named after the "sudden death" playoff that workingmen used to end their lunchtime dice games, it still has an unpretentious, working-class feel. The decor is simple, with wood tables, grimy yellow wallpaper, and some-other-era garland trim. Tiny metal plates on the  walls mark spots where gas-powered flames once flickered—used by patrons to light their cigars. A typical lunch or snack here is a *tartine* (open-face sandwich, €5) spread with *fromage blanc* (cream cheese) or pressed meat. Eat it with one of the home-brewed, *lambic*-based beers. This is a good place to try the *kriek* (cherry-flavored) beer. The Bruxelloise claim it goes well with sandwiches.

At **Le Cirio,** across from the Bourse, the dark tables bear the skid marks of over a century's worth of beer steins (nightly 10:00–1:00 in the morning, Rue de la Bourse 18–20, tel. 02-512-1395).

A la Bécasse is lower profile than Le Cirio, with a simple wood-panel and wood-table decor that appeals to both poor students and lunching businessmen. The home-brewed *lambic doux* has been served in clay jars since 1825. It's just around the corner from Le Cirio, toward the Grand Place, hidden away at the end of a courtyard (Mon–Sat 10:00–24:00, Sun 11:00–24:00, Rue de Tabora 11, tel. 02-511-0006).

Two Humble Bars: The classics recommended above are famous among tourists and understandably so. The following local hangouts offer a more basic, neighborhood feel: **Fin de Siècle** is a youthful bohemian scene serving basic, no-pretense Belgian/French dishes for around €13 (daily from 18:00, Rue des Chartreux 9). The adjacent **Le Greenwich** is a chess bar with a rough, circa-1900 former elegance serving good beer and simpler plates—like spaghetti (closed Sun, Rue des Chartreux 7, tel. 02-511-4167).

TRANSPORTATION CONNECTIONS

Belgium

Belgium's train system is slick, efficient, and non-smoking. Consider these rail deals for traveling within the country (www .b-rail.be):

- **Youths** under age 26 can get a Go Pass: €46 for 10 rides anywhere in Belgium (www.gopass.be).
- **Seniors** (age 65-plus) can get a same-day round-trip ticket to anywhere in Belgium for €4 (weekdays: after 9:00; weekends: no restrictions mid-Sept–April, not valid May–mid-Sept).
- Those traveling on the **weekend** should request the weekend discount for round-trips (50 percent off, valid Fri after 19:00). Note that if you have a bike, you'll pay extra to bring it on the train (€5 one-way, €8 round-trip).

Bruges

Trains

From Bruges by Train to: Brussels (2/hr, usually at :31 and :57, 1 hr, €12.30), **Ghent** (2/hr, 40 min), **Ostende** (3/hr, 15 min), **Köln** (6/ day, 3.5 hrs, change at Brussels Midi), **Paris** (1/day direct, about 2/ hr via Brussels, 2.5 hrs on fast Thalys trains—it's best to book by 20:00 the day before), **Amsterdam** (hourly, 3.5–4 hrs, transfer at Antwerp Central or Brussels Midi; transfer can be timed closely—be alert and check with conductor), **Amsterdam's Schiphol Airport** (hourly, 3.5 hrs, transfer in Antwerp or Brussels,), **Haarlem** (1–2/hr, 3.5 hrs, requires transfer). Train info: tel. 050/302-424.

    Trains from London: Bruges is an ideal "Welcome to Europe" stop after London. Take the Eurostar train from London to Brussels (10/day, 2.5 hrs), then transfer, backtracking to Bruges

TRANS CONN BELGIUM

Belgian Train Lines

(2/hr, 1 hr, entire trip is covered by same Eurostar ticket; see Eurostar details on next page).

Brussels

Trains

Brussels has three train stations: Central, Midi, and Nord. Be sure you're clear on which station or stations your train uses.

From Brussels by Train to: Bruges (2/hr, 1 hr; from any of Brussels' train stations, catch Intercity train—direction: Ostende or Knokke-Blankenberge, €12.30), **Amsterdam** (stopping at Amsterdam's Schiphol Airport on the way, hourly, 2.75 hrs, from Central, Midi, or Nord—sometimes from just one station, but sometimes all three), **Haarlem** (hourly, 2.75 hrs, transfer in Rotterdam), **Berlin** (7/day, 7.5–9 hrs, from Midi, transfer in Köln; can also transfer to night train in Köln), **Frankfurt** (9/day, 3.5 hrs direct from Midi or 5.5 hrs with transfer in Köln from Midi), **Munich** (9/day, 7–8.5 hrs; from Midi and Nord, most transfer in Köln or Frankfurt), **Rome** (3/day, 17 hrs; from Nord, transfer in

Milan, Zürich, or Paris), **Paris** (fast Thalys trains zip to Paris 2/hr, 1.5 hrs, from Midi—it's best to book by 20:00 the day before, or risk limited availability on same day). When booking Thalys (and similar express) trains to or from Paris, Amsterdam, and Köln, even railpass-holders need to pay the supplement of €14.50 for second class or €20 for first class. The first-class supplement generally gets you a meal on board. Train info: tel. 02-528-2828 (long wait), www.thalys.com.

By Eurostar to/from London: Brussels and London are two and a half hours apart by Eurostar train (10/day). Fares are reasonable but complicated. Prices vary depending on how far ahead you reserve, whether you can live with restrictions, and whether you're eligible for any discounts (children, youths, seniors, and railpass holders all qualify). Rates are lowest for round-trips.

Fares can change without notice, but typically a **one-way, full-fare ticket** (with no restrictions on refundability) runs about $425 first-class and $310 second-class. Accepting more restrictions lowers the price substantially (figure $90–200 for second class, one-way), but these **cheaper seats** sell out quickly. Those traveling with a railpass that covers Belgium or Britain should look first at the **passholder** fare (about $90–160 for second-class, one-way Eurostar trips). Eurostar tickets between London and Brussels include travel to/from any Belgian city at no additional cost within 24 hours of the Brussels Eurostar arrival or departure (not valid on Thalys express trains). Just show the Eurostar ticket when boarding the other train(s).

You can check the latest fares and book tickets by phone or online in the US (order online at www.ricksteves.com/rail/euro star.htm, prices listed in dollars; or order by phone at US tel. 800-EUROSTAR) or in Belgium (www.eurostar.com, prices listed in euros; Belgian tel. 02-528-2828). While tickets are usually cheaper if purchased in the US, fares offered in Europe follow different discount rules—so it can be worth it to check www.euro star.com before purchasing. If you buy from a US company, you'll pay for ticket delivery in the US. In Europe, you can buy your Eurostar ticket at any major train station in any country or at any travel agency that handles train tickets

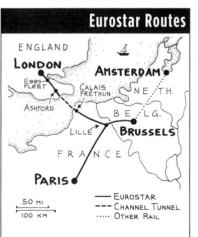

Eurostar Routes

ENGLAND
LONDON
EBBS-FLEET
ASHFORD
AMSTERDAM
CALAIS FRÉTHUN
NE TH.
BEL G.
LILLE
BRUSSELS
FRANCE
PARIS

50 MI
100 KM

—— EUROSTAR
- - - CHANNEL TUNNEL
····· OTHER RAIL

(expect a booking fee).

Trains to London leave from platforms #1 and #2 at Brussels Midi. Arrive 30 minutes early to get your ticket validated and your luggage and passport checked by British authorities (similar to an airport check-in for an international flight).

By Bus to: London (cost can vary, but generally €35 one-way, €70 round-trip, about 9 hrs, Eurolines tel. 02-203-0707 in Brussels, www.eurolines.com).

Airports

Brussels Airport

The clear winner for getting to and from the airport (nine miles from downtown Brussels) is the Airport Express shuttle train that runs from Brussels Midi and Central stations (€2.90, 4/hr, 25 min, daily 6:00–23:00). If you're connecting the airport with Bruges, take this shuttle train and transfer in Brussels. For a taxi, figure on spending €40 between downtown Brussels and the airport. Airport info: tel. 0900-70000, www.brusselsairport.be.

Brussels Airlines flies cheaply between Brussels and Athens, Milan, Rome, Florence, Geneva, Nice, Lisbon, Barcelona, Madrid, and more (Belgian tel. 07-035-1111, www.brusselsairlines .com). Bmi british midland has inexpensive flights from Brussels to London and the British Isles (www.flybmi.com). Non-discount airlines, such as Lufthansa (www.lufthansa.com), Finnair (www .finnair.com), and Alitalia (www.alitalia.com), offer daily flights from Brussels Airport.

Brussels South Charleroi Airport

Discount airlines Ryanair (www.ryanair.com) and Wizz Air (www.wizzair.com) use this smaller airport, located about 30 miles from downtown Brussels in the town of Gosselies. The airport is connected to Brussels Central Station by shuttle bus (runs hourly, 60 min, last shuttle at 22:30, www.voyages-lelan.com) and by train (bus #A connects Charleroi Airport and Charleroi Station—2/hr, 18 min; Charleroi-Brussels trains go 2/hr, 60 min). Airport info: tel. 07-125-1211, www.charleroi-airport.com.

PRACTICALITIES

This section covers just the basics on traveling in Belgium (for more information, see *Rick Steves' Amsterdam, Bruges & Brussels*). You can find free advice on specific topics at www.ricksteves.com/tips.

Money

Belgium uses the euro currency: 1 euro (€) = about $1.40. To convert prices in euros to dollars, add about 40 percent: €20 = about $28, €50 = about $70. (Check www.oanda.com for the latest exchange rates.)

The standard way for travelers to get euros is to withdraw money from a cash machine (called a *geldautomaat* in Flemish, or a *retrait* or *distributeur de billets* in French) using a debit or credit card, ideally with a Visa or MasterCard logo. Before departing, call your bank or credit-card company: Confirm that your card will work overseas, ask about international transaction fees, and alert them that you'll be making withdrawals in Europe.

To keep your valuables safe, wear a money belt. But if you do lose your credit or debit card, report the loss immediately to the respective global customer-assistance centers. Call these 24-hour US numbers collect: Visa (410/581-9994), MasterCard (636/722-7111), and American Express (623/492-8427).

Phoning

Smart travelers use the telephone to reserve or reconfirm rooms, reserve restaurants, get directions, research transportation connections, confirm tour times, phone home, and lots more.

To call Belgium from the US or Canada: Dial 011-32 and then the local number, minus its initial zero. (The 011 is our international access code, and 32 is Belgium's country code.)

To call Belgium from a European country: Dial 00-32 followed by the local number, minus its initial zero. (The 00 is Europe's international access code.)

To call within Belgium: Just dial the local number.

To call from Belgium to another country: Dial 00 followed by the country code (for example, 1 for the US or Canada), then the area code and number. If you're calling European countries whose phone numbers begin with 0, you'll usually have to omit that 0 when you dial.

Tips on Phoning: To make calls in Belgium, you can buy two different types of phone cards—international or insertable—sold locally at newsstands. Cheap international phone cards, which work with a scratch-to-reveal PIN code at any phone, allow you to call home to the US for pennies a minute, and also work for domestic calls within Belgium. Insertable phone cards, which must be inserted into public pay phones, are reasonable for calls within Belgium (and work for international calls as well, but not as cheaply as the international phone cards). Calling from your hotel-room phone is usually expensive, unless you use an international phone card. A mobile phone—whether an American one that works in Belgium, or a European one you buy when you arrive—is handy, but can be pricey. For more on phoning, see www.ricksteves.com/phoning.

Emergency Telephone Numbers in Belgium: For English-speaking **police** help, dial 101 or 112. To summon an **ambulance** or **fire truck,** call 100 or 112. For passport problems, call the **US Embassy** (in Brussels, tel. 02-508-2111; for after-hours emergencies, call and ask to be connected to the duty officer) or the **Canadian Embassy** (in Brussels, tel. 02-741-0611). For other concerns, get advice from your hotel.

Making Hotel Reservations

To ensure the best value, I recommend reserving rooms in advance, particularly during peak season. Email the hotelier with the following key pieces of information: number and type of rooms; number of nights; date of arrival; date of departure; and any special requests. (For a sample form, see www.ricksteves.com/reservation.) Use the European style for writing dates: day/month/year. For example, for a two-night stay in July, you could request: "1 double room for 2 nights, arrive 16/07/10, depart 18/07/10." Hoteliers typically ask for your credit-card number as a deposit.

In general, hotel prices can soften if you do any of the following: offer to pay cash, stay at least three nights, or travel at off-peak times (business-class hotels in Brussels often have discounts on weekends). You can also try asking for a cheaper room (for example, with a bathroom down the hall), or offer to skip breakfast.

Eating

Belgians have lunch around 12:00–14:00, and dinner—the biggest meal of the day—is eaten about 18:00–21:00.

In addition to restaurants, Belgium has other types of eateries. Cafés are all-purpose establishments, serving light meals at mealtimes, and coffee, drinks, and snacks at other times. An *eetcafé* is a simple restaurant serving basic, traditional meals in a straightforward setting. A *proeflokaal* is a bar (with snacks) for tasting wine, spirits, or beer. And there's no shortage of stand-up, take-out places serving Flemish fries, pickled herring, sandwiches, and all kinds of quick ethnic fare—including falafels (fried chickpea balls in pita bread), shoarmas (lamb tucked in pita bread), and *döner kebabs* (Turkish version of a shoarma).

Good service is relaxed (slow to an American). You won't get the bill until you ask for it. Most restaurants include a 15 percent service charge in their prices, but an additional tip of about 5-10 percent is a nice reward for good service. In bars, rounding up to the next euro ("keep the change") is appropriate if you get table service, but not necessary if you order at the bar.

For more on Belgian food (and beer), see the Bruges Eating and Nightlife chapter.

Transportation

By Train: Hourly trains connect Bruges and Brussels faster and easier than driving. Just buy tickets as you go. You don't need advance reservations to ride a train between these cities. If you're coming from Amsterdam, note that the Amsterdam–Brussels Thalys train is pricey but avoidable; plenty of regular trains also make this run. To research train schedules, visit Germany's excellent all-Europe website, http://bahn.hafas.de/bin/query.exe/en, or Belgium's www.b-rail.be. For more extensive travels beyond Belgium, you may want to study your railpass options (see www. ricksteves.com/rail). For more specifics, see the Transportation Connections chapter.

By Car: It's cheaper to arrange most car rentals from the US. For tips on your insurance options, see www.ricksteves.com/cdw. Bring your driver's license. For route planning, try www.viamichelin.com. A car is a worthless headache in cities (including Bruges and Brussels)—get tips from your hotel on where to park safely.

Helpful Hints

Time: Belgium uses the 24-hour clock. It's the same through 12:00 noon, then keep going: 13:00, 14:00, and so on. Belgium, like most of continental Europe, is six/nine hours ahead of the East/West Coasts of the US.

PRACTICALITIES

Holidays and Festivals: Belgium celebrates many holidays, which can close sights and attract crowds (book hotel rooms ahead). For information on holidays and festivals, check Belgium's website: www.visitbelgium.com. For a simple list showing major—though not all—events, see www.ricksteves.com/festivals.

Numbers and Stumblers: What Americans call the second floor of a building is the first floor in Europe. Europeans write dates as day/month/year, so Christmas is 25/12/10. Commas are decimal points and vice versa—a dollar and a half is 1,50, and there are 5.280 feet in a mile. Belgium uses the metric system: A kilogram is 2.2 pounds; a liter is about a quart; and a kilometer is six-tenths of a mile.

Language: Belgium is linguistically divided. The northern part of the country (including Bruges) speaks Flemish. The southern part of the country (including Brussels) speaks French. Many people throughout the country also speak English. But just in case, I've included both Flemish and French survival phrases in this chapter.

Resources from Rick Steves

This Snapshot guide is excerpted from *Rick Steves' Amsterdam, Bruges & Brussels* 7th edition, which is one of more than 30 titles in my series of guidebooks on European travel. I also produce a public television series, *Rick Steves' Europe*, and a public radio show, *Travel with Rick Steves*. My website, www.ricksteves.com, offers free travel information, free vodcasts and podcasts of my shows, free audio tours of major sights in Europe (for you to download onto an iPod or other MP3 player), a Graffiti Wall for travelers' comments, guidebook updates, my travel blog, an online travel store, and information on European railpasses and our tours of Europe.

Additional Resources

Tourist Information: www.visitbelgium.com
Passports and Red Tape: www.travel.state.gov
Packing List: www.ricksteves.com/packlist
Cheap Flights: www.skyscanner.net
Airplane Carry-on Restrictions: www.tsa.gov/travelers
Updates for This Book: www.ricksteves.com/update.

How Was Your Trip?

If you'd like to share your tips, concerns, and discoveries after using this book, please fill out the survey at www.ricksteves.com/feedback. Thanks in advance—it helps a lot.

Flemish Survival Phrases

Northern Belgium speaks Flemish—closely related to Dutch. You won't need to learn Flemish, but knowing a few phrases can help. Taking a few moments to learn the pleasantries (such as please and thank you) will improve your connections with locals.

To pronounce the difficult Flemish "g" (indicated in phonetics by hhh), make a hard, guttural, clear-your-throat sound, similar to the "ch" in the Scottish word "loch."

Hello.	**Hallo.**	hol-LOH
Good day.	**Dag.**	dahhh
Good morning.	**Goeiemorgen.**	hhhoy-ah-MOR-hhhen
Good afternoon.	**Goeiemiddag.**	hhhoy-ah-MIT-tahk
Ma'am	**Mevrouw**	meh-frow
Sir	**Meneer**	men-ear
Yes	**Ja**	yah
No	**Nee**	nay
Please	**Alstublieft**	AHL-stoo-bleeft
Thank you.	**Dank u wel.**	dahnk yoo vehl
You're welcome.	**Graag gedaan.**	hhhrahhk hhkeh-dahn
Excuse me.	**Pardon.**	par-DOHN
Do you speak English?	**Spreekt u Engels?**	spraykt oo ENG-els
Okay.	**Oké.**	"okay"
Goodbye.	**Tot ziens.**	toht zeens
one / two	**een / twee**	ayn / t'vay
three / four	**drie / vier**	dree / feer
five / six	**vijf / zes**	fife / ses
seven / eight	**zeven / acht**	say-fen / ahkht
nine / ten	**negen / tien**	nay-hhhen / teen
What does it cost?	**Wat kost?**	vaht kost
I would like...	**Ik wil graag...**	ik vil hhhrahhhk
...a room.	**...een kamer.**	un kah-mer
...a ticket.	**...een kaart.**	un kart
...a bike.	**...een fiets.**	un feets
Where is...?	**Waar is...?**	vahr is
...the station	**...het station**	het sta-tsee-on
...the tourist info office	**...de VVV**	duh vay vay vay
left / right	**links / rechts**	links / rechts
open / closed	**open / gesloten**	"open" / hhhe-sloh-ten

In the Restaurant

The Belgians have an all-purpose word, *alstublieft* (AHL-stoo-bleeft), that means: "Please" or "Here you are" (if handing you something), or "Thanks" (if taking payment from you), or "You're welcome" (when handing change). Here are other words that might come in handy at restaurants:

I would like...	**Ik wil graag...**	ik vil hhhrahhk
...a cup of coffee.	**...kopje koffee.**	kop-yeh "coffee"
non-smoking	**niet-roken**	neet roh-ken
smoking	**roken**	roh-ken
with / without	**met / buiten**	met / bow-ten
and / or	**en / of**	en / of
bread	**brood**	broht
salad	**sla**	slah
cheese	**kaas**	kahs
meat	**vlees**	flays
chicken	**kip**	kip
fish	**vis**	fis
egg	**ei**	eye
fruit	**vrucht**	frucht
pastries	**gebak**	hhhe-bak
I am vegetarian.	**Ik ben vegetarish.**	ik ben vay-hhhe-tah-rish
Tasty.	**Lekker.**	lek-ker
Enjoy!	**Smakelijk!**	smak-kuh-luk
Cheers!	**Proost!**	prohst

French Survival Phrases

When using the phonetics, try to nasalize the n̲ sound.

Good day.	**Bonjour.**	boh̲n-zhoor
Mrs. / Mr.	**Madame / Monsieur**	mah-dahm / muhs-yur
Do you speak English?	**Parlez-vous anglais?**	par-lay-voo ah̲n-glay
Yes. / No.	**Oui. / Non.**	wee / noh̲n
I understand.	**Je comprends.**	zhuh koh̲n-prahn
I don't understand.	**Je ne comprends pas.**	zhuh nuh koh̲n-prahn pah
Please.	**S'il vous plaît.**	see voo play
Thank you.	**Merci.**	mehr-see
I'm sorry.	**Désolé.**	day-zoh-lay
Excuse me.	**Pardon.**	par-doh̲n
(No) problem.	**(Pas de) problème.**	(pah duh) proh-blehm
It's good.	**C'est bon.**	say boh̲n
Goodbye.	**Au revoir.**	oh vwahr
one / two	**un / deux**	uh̲n / duh
three / four	**trois / quatre**	twah / kah-truh
five / six	**cinq / six**	sa̲nk / sees
seven / eight	**sept / huit**	seht / weet
nine / ten	**neuf / dix**	nuhf / dees
How much is it?	**Combien?**	koh̲n-bee-a̲n
Write it?	**Ecrivez?**	ay-kree-vay
Is it free?	**C'est gratuit?**	say grah-twee
Included?	**Inclus?**	a̲n-klew
Where can I buy / find...?	**Où puis-je acheter / trouver...?**	oo pwee-zhuh ah-shuh-tay / troo-vay
I'd like / We'd like...	**Je voudrais / Nous voudrions...**	zhuh voo-dray / noo voo-dree-oh̲n
...a room.	**...une chambre.**	ewn shah̲n-bruh
...a ticket to ___.	**...un billet pour ___.**	uh̲n bee-yay poor
Is it possible?	**C'est possible?**	say poh-see-bluh
Where is...?	**Où est...?**	oo ay
...the train station	**...la gare**	lah gar
...the bus station	**...la gare routière**	lah gar root-yehr
...tourist information	**...l'office du tourisme**	loh-fees dew too-reez-muh
Where are the toilets?	**Où sont les toilettes?**	oo soh̲n lay twah-leht
men	**hommes**	ohm
women	**dames**	dahm
left / right	**à gauche / à droite**	ah gohsh / ah dwaht
straight	**tout droit**	too dwah
When does this open / close?	**Ça ouvre / ferme à quelle heure?**	sah oo-vruh / fehrm ah kehl ur
At what time?	**À quelle heure?**	ah kehl ur
Just a moment.	**Un moment.**	uh̲n moh-mah̲n
now / soon / later	**maintenant / bientôt / plus tard**	ma̲n-tuh-nah̲n / bee-a̲n-toh / plew tar
today / tomorrow	**aujourd'hui / demain**	oh-zhoor-dwee / duh-ma̲n

PRACTICALITIES

In the Restaurant

I'd like / We'd like...	**Je voudrais / Nous voudrions...**	zhuh voo-dray / noo voo-dree-ohn
...to reserve...	**...réserver...**	ray-zehr-vay
...a table for one / two.	**...une table pour un / deux.**	ewn tah-bluh poor uhn / duh
Non-smoking.	**Non fumeur.**	nohn few-mur
Is this seat free?	**C'est libre?**	say lee-bruh
The menu (in English), please.	**La carte (en anglais),** s'il vous plaît.	lah kart (ahn ahn-glay) see voo play
service (not) included	**service (non) compris**	sehr-vees (nohn) kohn-pree
to go	**à emporter**	ah ahn-por-tay
with / without	**avec / sans**	ah-vehk / sahn
and / or	**et / ou**	ay / oo
special of the day	**plat du jour**	plah dew zhoor
specialty of the house	**spécialité de la maison**	spay-see-ah-lee-tay duh lah may-zohn
appetizers	**hors-d'oeuvre**	or-duh-vruh
first course (soup, salad)	**entrée**	ahn-tray
main course (meat, fish)	**plat principal**	plah pran-see-pahl
bread	**pain**	pan
cheese	**fromage**	froh-mahzh
sandwich	**sandwich**	sahnd-weech
soup	**soupe**	soop
salad	**salade**	sah-lahd
meat	**viande**	vee-ahnd
chicken	**poulet**	poo-lay
fish	**poisson**	pwah-sohn
seafood	**fruits de mer**	frwee duh mehr
fruit	**fruit**	frwee
vegetables	**légumes**	lay-gewm
dessert	**dessert**	duh-sehr
mineral water	**eau minérale**	oh mee-nay-rahl
tap water	**l'eau du robinet**	loh dew roh-bee-nay
milk	**lait**	lay
(orange) juice	**jus (d'orange)**	zhew (doh-rahnzh)
coffee	**café**	kah-fay
tea	**thé**	tay
wine	**vin**	van
red / white	**rouge / blanc**	roozh / blahn
glass / bottle	**verre / bouteille**	vehr / boo-teh-ee
beer	**bière**	bee-ehr
Cheers!	**Santé!**	sahn-tay
More. / Another.	**Plus. / Un autre.**	plew / uhn oh-truh
The same.	**La même chose.**	lah mehm shohz
The bill, please.	**L'addition, s'il vous plaît.**	lah-dee-see-ohn see voo play
tip	**pourboire**	poor-bwar
Delicious!	**Délicieux!**	day-lee-see-uh

For more user-friendly French phrases, check out *Rick Steves' French Phrase Book and Dictionary* or *Rick Steves' French, Italian & German Phrase Book*.

▸ Plan Your Trip

Browse thousands of articles and a wealth of money-saving tips for planning your dream trip. You'll find up-to-date information on Europe's best destinations, packing smart, getting around, finding rooms, staying healthy, avoiding scams and more.

▸ Eurail Passes

Find out, step-by-step, if a rail pass makes sense for your trip—and how to avoid buying more than you need. Get a bunch of free extras!

▸ Graffiti Wall & Travelers' Helpline

Learn, ask, share—our online community of savvy travelers is a great resource for first-time travelers to Europe, as well as seasoned pros.

Rick Steves' Europe Through the Back Door, Inc

Rick Steves

www.ricksteves.com

TRAVEL SKILLS
Europe Through the Back Door

EUROPE GUIDES
Best of Europe
Eastern Europe
Europe 101
European Christmas
Postcards from Europe

COUNTRY GUIDES
Croatia & Slovenia
England
France
Germany
Great Britain
Ireland
Italy
Portugal
Scandinavia
Spain
Switzerland

CITY & REGIONAL GUIDES
Amsterdam, Bruges & Brussels
Athens & The Peloponnese
Budapest
Florence & Tuscany
Istanbul
London
Paris
Prague & The Czech Republic
Provence & The French Riviera
Rome
Venice
Vienna, Salzburg & Tirol

PHRASE BOOKS & DICTIONARIES
French
French, Italian & German
German
Italian
Portuguese
Spanish

RICK STEVES' EUROPE DVDs
Austria & The Alps
Eastern Europe
England
Europe
France & Benelux
Germany & Scandinavia
Greece, Turkey, Israel & Egypt
Ireland & Scotland
Italy's Cities
Italy's Countryside
Rick Steves' European Christmas
Spain & Portugal
Travel Skills & "The Making Of"

PLANNING MAPS
Britain, Ireland & London
Europe
France & Paris
Germany, Austria & Switzerland
Ireland
Italy
Spain & Portugal

JOURNALS
Rick Steves' Pocket Travel Journal
Rick Steves' Travel Journal

NOW AVAILABLE

RICK STEVES APPS FOR THE iPHONE OR iPOD TOUCH

With these apps you can:

▶ Spin the compass icon to switch views between sights, hotels, and restaurant selections—and get details on cost, hours, address, and phone number.

▶ Tap any point on the screen to read Rick's detailed information, including history and suggested viewpoints.

▶ Get a deeper view into Rick's tours with audio and video segments.

Go to iTunes to download the following apps:

Rick Steves' Louvre Tour

Rick Steves' Historic Paris Walk

Rick Steves' Orsay Museum Tour

Rick Steves' Versailles

Rick Steves' Ancient Rome Tour

Rick Steves' St. Peter's Basilica Tour

Once downloaded, these apps are completely self-contained on your iPhone or iPod Touch, so you will not incur pricey roaming charges during use overseas.

Rick Steves books and DVDs are available at bookstores and through online booksellers.

Rick Steves guidebooks are published by Avalon Travel, a member of the Perseus Books Group.

Rick Steves apps are produced by Übermind, a boutique Seattle-based software consultancy firm.

Avalon Travel
a member of the Perseus Books Group
1700 Fourth Street
Berkeley, CA 94710, USA

Printed in the U.S.A. by Worzalla
First printing August 2009

Portions of this book were originally published in *Rick Steves' France* © 2006, 2005, 2004,
2003, 2002 by Rick Steves and Steve Smith.

ISBN: 978-1-59880-484-3

For the latest on Rick's lectures, books, tours, public radio show, and public television series,
contact Europe Through the Back Door, Box 2009, Edmonds, WA 98020, tel. 425/771-
8303, fax 425/771-0833, www.ricksteves.com, rick@ricksteves.com.

Europe Through the Back Door Senior Editor: Jennifer Madison Davis
ETBD Editors: Cameron Hewitt, Tom Griffin, Cathy McDonald, Sarah McCormic
ETBD Managing Editor: Risa Laib
Avalon Travel Senior Editor & Series Manager: Madhu Prasher
Avalon Travel Project Editor: Kelly Lydick
Copy Editor: Judith Brown
Proofreader: Ellie Behrstock
Production & Typesetting: McGuire Barber Design
Cover Design: Kimberly Glyder Design
Maps and Graphics: David C. Hoerlein, Laura VanDeventer, Lauren Mills, Pat O'Connor,
    Barb Geisler, Mike Morgenfeld
Photography: Rick Steves, Dominic Bonuccelli, Gene Openshaw, Jennifer Hauseman,
    Laura VanDeventer, Bruce VanDeventer
Cover Photo: Bruges Market Square © Amelia Brown/bigstockphoto.com

*Although the author and publisher have made every effort to provide accurate, up-to-date
information, they accept no responsibility for loss, injury, bad herring, or inconvenience sustained
by any person using this book.*

ABOUT THE AUTHORS

RICK STEVES

Rick Steves is on a mission: to help make European travel accessible and meaningful for Americans. Rick has spent four months every year since 1973 exploring Europe. He's researched and written more than 30 travel guidebooks, writes and hosts the public television series *Rick Steves' Europe*, and also produces and hosts the weekly public radio show *Travel with Rick Steves.* With the help of his hardworking staff of 70 at Europe Through the Back Door, Rick organizes tours of Europe and offers an information-packed website (www. ricksteves.com). Rick, his wife (and favorite travel partner) Anne, and their two teenage children, Andy and Jackie, call Edmonds, just north of Seattle, home.

GENE OPENSHAW

Gene Openshaw is a writer, composer, tour guide, and lecturer on art and history. Specializing in writing walking tours of Europe's cultural sights, Gene has co-authored seven of Rick's books and contributes to Rick's public television series. As a composer, Gene has written a full-length opera *(Matter)*, a violin sonata, and dozens of songs. He lives near Seattle with his daughter, and roots for the Mariners in good times and bad.